Opening up

Job

IAN S. MCNAUGHTON

DayOne

Opening up
Job
IAN S. MCNAUGHTON

Revd McNaughton has given us a journey through Job that is both accessible and deeply enriching. Not only does this commentary capture the main themes of God's sovereignty and providence, but it does so in a way that continually points out God's work of sanctifying grace in the Christian life. Most importantly, our attention is continually directed towards Job's Redeemer, who indeed lives.

Steve Ham, Senior Director, Answers in Genesis Worldwide

Job is undoubtedly one of the most important books ever written; that is why this well-organized mini-commentary by Ian McNaughton does many of us a service. It gives the reader easy access to the way the Book of Job develops beyond the familiar first

two chapters. And it does this without missing the theological beat that is contained therein. Big questions and big themes are laid bare for us to consider, with some excellent questions for discussion and further study helpfully placed at the end of each chapter.
One of the most refreshing things for the spiritually thirsty reader is the way that Ian McNaughton sets before us what might rightly be called 'The gospel according to Saint Job'. I heartily recommend this guide to a great book. I thought it was excellent and thoroughly enjoyed reading it.

Shaun Thompson, pastor and church-planter in Albania with AEM

The Book of Job is a difficult book to understand, consisting largely of attempts by well-meaning friends to provide counselling advice on Job's many problems associated with human

suffering. While representing genuine
attempts to be helpful, they are wrong
diagnoses of the cause of his problems.
Because of this, the Book of Job is
usually daunting to the Christian reader
and regularly misunderstood.

This volume provides a clear and
reliable introductory guide enabling
the reader to grasp the thrust of the
various arguments while at the same
time showing where they fall short.
It is of practical value as it outlines
where the arguments may be validly
applied in other situations and identifies
principles for the reader to consider
and further develop. It also seeks
to direct the reader to the ultimate
example in suffering, our Lord and
Saviour Jesus Christ, with whom Job
has many things in common. It has an
interesting section dealing with the
behemoth, which it identifies with a
dinosaur, and Leviathan, which it links

with Antichrist and the return of Jesus Christ. Ian McNaughton has read widely and this volume is a useful and concise introductory guide to a very important treatise on the problem of suffering within the providence of God.

Dr Robert Beckett B.Agr., M.S., Ph.D., Dip.Th., minister of the Evangelical Presbyterian Church in North Belfast

The wise Bible-reader welcomes help on the Book of Job, especially since Job's experiences of suffering can touch our own lives. This new study on Job by Ian McNaughton has several appealing qualities. The author has a high view of the Bible's divine inspiration, he has a sound biblical theology and he throws light on what all acknowledge to be a difficult book of the Bible. Christians, like others, can suffer pain and loss in this life. The author exposes the error of imagining that a Christian's sufferings are necessarily to be viewed as God's punishment for secret sin. A helpful addition to the commentary is an insight into aspects of the Book of Job which relate to creationism. Job, we learn, lived in the age not only of patriarchs, but also of dinosaurs. This new study will throw welcome light on a profound book of Holy Scripture.

Revd Maurice Roberts, Free Church of Scotland (Continuing)

Job is a fascinating book and is probably the oldest book in the Bible. Ian McNaughton guides the reader through it in a masterful way, showing the main points to look for in each section. With the unusual and difficult providence that fell to Job, the lessons of this book are so relevant to all in every generation and very pertinent today, as many grope in great difficulty seeking the answers for their own lives. Ian brings these lessons from Job carefully into focus at the end

of each chapter with very pertinent
questions for the reader.

Of particular interest also are the
statements on creation which run through
the book—notably at the end (Job 40),
when the Lord refers to a list of creatures
as he speaks to Job. Ian rightly indicates
(ch. 12) that the description of the
behemoth is likely to be that of a long-
necked sauropod dinosaur which Job
knew of in his day. Job therefore has much
to teach us in this day of evolutionary
philosophy passed off as science.

Professor A. C. McIntosh, Leeds

I am delighted to have read this excellent
study on the Book of Job. As a creation
speaker, I found the expositions of God's
discourse to Job about his creation
to be particularly valuable. Accurate
creationist descriptions of the behemoth
and Leviathan are seldom found in
conjunction with a good commentary on

the whole book. Ian McNaughton has achieved this feat splendidly, so I heartily recommend the book.

Paul Taylor, B.Sc., M.Ed., Director of Ministry Development, Creation Today, Pensacola, FL, USA

In the opening paragraph of the Overview, Ian writes, 'The Book of Job ... is one of a few books in Holy Scripture that are out of reach for all except the most diligent of students. I present this work as an introduction in the hope that it will encourage more study.' On that basis, Ian has done an excellent job. This book is easy to read and gives the Bible student a much-needed understanding that suffering is a part of human experience, both for the believer and the non-believer; no one is immune. He shows how, from our human perspective, it is often a mistake to try to make sense of particular instances of suffering; that certainly we should be wary of making judgements; and that, despite appearances, we can be sure that God is not indifferent to our plight.

It is great to see how Ian also opens the Bible student up to the bigger picture of suffering, going beyond the limitations of Job or our own suffering by connecting the story of Job to the Lord Jesus himself, who, like Job but to a greater degree, was considered forsaken by God, under God's judgement, but later vindicated, becoming the intercessor for his accusers.

Ian has helpfully included questions and discussion points at the end of each chapter. This makes the book useful for small-group or one-to-one study. I look forward to using it as a tool for discipling new believers.

Julian Rebera, Pastor, New Life Church, Brighton, East Sussex

As a Christian of many years and a
leader in the church of Jesus Christ, I've
often wrestled with the question of why
the righteous are so often called on to
suffer. This book has enabled me to see
this issue, not from man's perspective,
but from God's. Fellowship with God,
and the blessings that flow from having
God at the centre of our lives, give us
a right perspective. Job's 'comforters'
and his wife all looked on from a human
perspective, but a truly meek Christian
will seek first the will and ways of God
over his or her own comforts, knowing
that whatever God has ordained for us,
he is working all towards our ultimate
good (Rom. 8:28).

**Revd Steve Packham, Southern Cross Evangelical Church,
Portslade, East Sussex**

Ian McNaughton has written a very
helpful and well-written introduction
to the book of Job that is surprisingly

thorough with many helpful references. He shows from the example of Job why it is wrong to be angry with God about our circumstances. He gives some very interesting insights into some of the creatures found in the Book of Job, such as Leviathan and the behemoth. The book applies lessons to everyday life, especially concerning our attitude and our response to suffering and hard times. In a world that desires instant pleasures and instant solutions, there is a need today for contentment and patience. This book encourages such godly attitudes.

Professor Stuart Burgess, B.Sc.(Eng.), Ph.D., C.Eng., F.I.Mech.E.

First printed 2014

Unless otherwise indicated, Scripture quotations are from the New King James Version (NKJV)®. Copyright © 1982 by Thomas Nelson, Inc. Used by permission. All rights reserved.

ISBN 978-1-84625-438-3

British Library Cataloguing in Publication Data available
Published by Day One Publications
Ryelands Road, Leominster, England, HR6 8NZ
TEL 01568 613 740 FAX 01568 611 473
email—sales@dayone.co.uk
UK web site—www.dayone.co.uk
All rights reserved.

Printed by TJ International

Dedication
To Mark, my only son,
and Olga, his wife,
two great people, and friends
in Christ Jesus our Lord

List of Bible abbreviations

THE OLD TESTAMENT		1 Chr.	1 Chronicles	Dan.	Daniel
		2 Chr.	2 Chronicles	Hosea	Hosea
Gen.	Genesis	Ezra	Ezra	Joel	Joel
Exod.	Exodus	Neh.	Nehemiah	Amos	Amos
Lev.	Leviticus	Esth.	Esther	Obad.	Obadiah
Num.	Numbers	Job	Job	Jonah	Jonah
Deut.	Deuteronomy	Ps.	Psalms	Micah	Micah
Josh.	Joshua	Prov.	Proverbs	Nahum	Nahum
Judg.	Judges	Eccles.	Ecclesiastes	Hab.	Habakkuk
Ruth	Ruth	S.of S.	Song of Solomon	Zeph.	Zephaniah
1 Sam.	1 Samuel	Isa.	Isaiah	Hag.	Haggai
2 Sam.	2 Samuel	Jer.	Jeremiah	Zech.	Zechariah
1 Kings	1 Kings	Lam.	Lamentations	Mal.	Malachi
2 Kings	2 Kings	Ezek.	Ezekiel		

THE NEW TESTAMENT		Gal.	Galatians	Heb.	Hebrews
		Eph.	Ephesians	James	James
Matt.	Matthew	Phil.	Philippians	1 Peter	1 Peter
Mark	Mark	Col.	Colossians	2 Peter	2 Peter
Luke	Luke	1 Thes.	1 Thessalonians	1 John	1 John
John	John	2 Thes.	2 Thessalonians	2 John	2 John
Acts	Acts	1 Tim.	1 Timothy	3 John	3 John
Rom.	Romans	2 Tim.	2 Timothy	Jude	Jude
1 Cor.	1 Corinthians	Titus	Titus	Rev.	Revelation
2 Cor.	2 Corinthians	Philem.	Philemon		

Contents

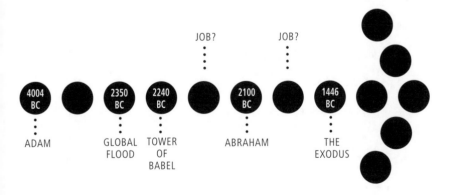

Overview

Most of the Bible's sixty-six books are read and understood by the majority of believers. The Book of Job, however, is one of a few books in Holy Scripture that are out of reach for all except the most diligent of students. I present this work as an introduction in the hope that it will encourage more study. I personally have been greatly blessed during my study, preaching and preparation of this book, and I trust that all readers will profit likewise.

The chief characters of the Book of Job appear in Job 1–2. They are (in the order in which they appear) Job, God, Satan, and Job's three 'friends' Eliphaz the Temanite, Bildad the Shuhite and Zophar the Naamathite. A fourth friend, Elihu, comes along later (chs 32–37). The book is not a story in the sense of a fable, legend or parable; rather it is a historical biography that traces Job's spiritual journey through bereavement and illness after he was justified by faith in the sight of God: 'Have you considered My servant Job, that there is none like him on the earth, a blameless and upright man, one who fears God and shuns evil?' (2:3).

I have chosen to limit this small introduction to the main themes expressed by Job himself and have left the longer sections, such as the addresses of Job's three friends and Elihu, for the reader's further study. At the end of each chapter, I have included questions to think about and suggestions for further study to help the reader get to grips with the message of the book. Those who wish to go deeper will find recommendations of more substantial works in the 'Additional Resources' section at the back of the book.

This Old Testament book has been popular with great preachers. The magisterial Reformer John Calvin preached 156 sermons from the Book of Job, and the famous Charles H. Spurgeon some 88 sermons. Very large commentaries have been written on Job. One manuscript containing nearly three hundred pages covers only Job 29–31, and a two-volume commentary will, when complete, contain nearly two million words.[1]

The questions discussed by Job and his friends are similar to the questions many people wrestle with today. Why is it that bad things happen to good people? Why me? Can suffering serve any good purpose? The New Testament assures God's people that suffering is not worthless or needless. The Book of Job helps us with possible solutions to these and other 'hot potato' issues and is given to show us that sickness and suffering are not always inevitably linked to personal sin.

> The New Testament assures God's people that suffering is not worthless or needless.

This commentary takes a high view of the text on which the Old Testament is based, believing that the autographs were written by holy men of God inspired by the Holy Spirit (2 Peter 1:21). We are grateful to God for the preservation of the text whose transmission has, we believe, been superintended by the Holy Spirit throughout the ages. Thus the Book of Job is 'profitable for doctrine, for reproof, ... for instruction in righteousness' and is able to make us wise for salvation through faith which is in Jesus Christ (2 Tim. 3:15–16). Being fixed for ever in the Old Testament canon, Job remains God's Word, and no amount of questioning its inspiration or authorship will alter this. We are thankful that it possesses the following two great marks of inspiration:

- 'The authority of the Holy Scripture, for which it ought to be believed and obeyed, depends not upon the testimony of any man or Church, but wholly upon God (who is truth itself), the Author thereof; and therefore it is to be received, because it is the Word of God.'
- '... our full persuasion and assurance of the infallible truth and divine authority thereof, ... from the inward work of the Holy Spirit bearing witness by and with the Word in our hearts.'[2]

One of the unique aspects of the Book of Job are the portions of scientific interest. Several of its chapters increase our understanding of supernatural creation and the secrets of the universe. These portions are so numerous that the book is regarded as a prime source of information on issues such as cosmology (chs 9, 26, 38), the hydrologic cycle (chs 26, 28, 37), geology (ch. 38) and astronomy (chs 9, 38). These will be looked at as is pertinent in a small introductory commentary to the book.

It is to be noted that Job reckoned it a privilege beyond understanding that the God of creation and eternity should be involved in his life and be committed to his personal well-being. This belief and trust shine through the book, despite the trial of faith Job experienced and the doubts he expressed in dialogue with his friends. Charles H. Spurgeon noted, 'If you are depressed, read the entire book of Job.

Some of Job's remarks were terrible, but who could doubt Job's salvation or his redemption? Today his name is one of the most illustrious of those who have overcome the world by faith.'[3]

Background and summary

The Book of Job is one of three great poetical books of the
Old Testament, Psalms and Proverbs being the other two.
They lie in the third division of the Old Testament canon
called the Hagiographa (the other two divisions are the Law
and the Prophets). Despite their poetic form they are didactic
in nature and are intended to teach us about God and about
ourselves. Each line of the Book of Job is limited to three or
four major words, with the second line of each pair essentially
saying the same as the first line but using different words for
clarification and emphasis. This is called 'line parallelism'.
The various English Bibles have marked differences in
translation because of the difficulty of rare words within the
Hebrew text.[1]

The book takes its title from its main character,
Iyyou—Job. That Job was a historical person needs to be
taken into account when handling the text; failure to do so
(by treating him as fictional) results in missing the point of
the book. In Islam, Job is called *Ayyûb* and his genealogy
is confused as he is reckoned to be either Isaac's or Lot's
grandson, or the great-great grandson of Esau.[2] The Koran's
comments on Job are obviously derived from the biblical text
but are mixed up with the story of Naaman (2 Kings 5). The
Koran tells us that Job's wife was beaten by him for having
listened to Satan (*Iblis*).[3]

Job is described as a man living in 'the land of Uz' (Job
1:1) and the 'greatest of all the people of the East' (1:3). The
location of Uz is unknown. Some have concluded that it was
in Syria or north-west Mesopotamia, but it may be related

to Aram in the north of the region (Gen. 10:22–23), where Abraham's nephew and family lived (Gen. 22:21), or to a descendant of Seir who lived alongside the sons of Esau in the land also referred to as Edom (Gen. 36:28). Uz may therefore be a name for a region in Edom, because many of the proper names in the Book of Job occur in the genealogy of Esau, the father of the Edomites (see Gen. 36; Jer. 25:20; Lam. 4:21).

Authorship and date

There is some divergence among commentators as to who wrote the Book of Job and when. Suggestions for an author include Job himself, Elihu (his fourth friend), and Moses; if you are interested in this issue, please consult the works listed in the 'Additional Resources' section at the back of this book. Any view that would divide the Book of Job into different eras must be rejected. Alfred Edersheim comments, 'Its scene and actors are laid in patriarchal times, and outside the family or immediate ancestry of Abraham. It is a story of Gentile life in the times of the earliest patriarchs. And yet anything more noble, grand, devout or spiritual than what the book contains is not found, "no, not in Israel".'[4]

Although the date and authorship of the book are unclear, this does not negate the view that it is inspired Scripture. To deny the Book of Job this honour is churlish and goes against tradition. There are helpful clues in the book as to when Job lived. 'There are certain indications in the narrative which seem to point to a time before the giving of the Sinaitic legislation. The patriarchal description in Job chapter 1 seems to support this.'[5] Clues in the text place Job around the patriarchal period in history.[6]

- Job's wealth is measured in terms of livestock, as is Abraham's and Jacob's.
- The phrase 'there is none like him on the earth' (1:8) would seem to place Job as living earlier than Abraham or just after Abraham's death. I take it to mean that Job became a believer *before* Abraham was born. That Job was the greatest among the people of the East (1:3) adds weight to his pre-Abrahamic existence.
- Job offered sacrifices to God in a patriarchal fashion (1:5).
- Job's longevity (42:16) is consistent with the lifespans of the patriarchs.
- The Hebrew word translated 'piece of silver' in 42:11 is also found in Genesis 33:19, in connection with the patriarch Jacob.
- The absence of the mention of any distinctive Israelitish institutions seems to point to a time before the giving of the Law at Sinai.

Why was the Book of Job written?

Evangelical theologians do not agree on the purpose of the Book of Job. Yet some things are clear. The Book of Job was written …

- To show that there is not an inevitable link between individual sin and personal suffering.
- To reveal the true character of God.
- As a clear guide to God's sovereign character in his dealings with this world in terms of justice, wisdom and grace.

- To expose the reality of Satan and satanic power.
- To comfort the people of God during their pilgrimage and to give hope for the journey.
- To encourage the people of God to trust him at all times.

The questions 'Why me?' and 'Why now?' are often on the lips of God's people in times of trial and suffering. Yet suffering is not always punishment for sins committed. The Bible is clear on this. 'The answer that the book of Job gives is that suffering is not related to anything particular that we have done: its reason is for some inscrutable divine purpose.'[7] It is our response to suffering that is important, and Job helps us to react well when it is our turn.

How did Job know that there is a God?

The monotheistic beliefs of Job and his companions are seen throughout the book. There is no hint of pantheism, polytheism, idolatry or evolutionism in the thoughts of the main characters. These errors crept into the hearts of fallen men and women after the flood and after the diaspora of the peoples at the tower of Babel.[8]

Divine laws were given to humankind long before the Ten Commandments and Moses. We are told that 'Abraham obeyed My voice and kept My charge, My commandments, My statutes, and My laws' (Gen. 26:5; Ps. 105:42). The knowledge of God and his precepts was passed down orally and then committed to writing. Job was conscious of knowing God's commandments, and it is also clear that he knew about God's way of reconciliation (Job 1:5; 42:7–9; compare Gen. 4:4; 8:20). The covenantal name of Yahweh/

TABLE OF SPEECHES

JOB CHAPTER/S	CHARACTER/S	COMMENT
1–2	God & Satan	behind the scenes activity & dialogue
3	Job	first speech
4–5	Eliphaz	first speech
6–7	Job	second speech
8	Bildad	first speech
9–10	Job	third speech
11	Zophar	first speech
12–14	Job	fourth speech
15	Eliphaz	second speech
16–17	Job	fifth speech
18	Bildad	second speech
19	Job	sixth speech
20	Zophar	second speech
21	Job	seventh speech
22	Eliphaz	third speech
23–24	Job	eighth speech
25	Bildad	third speech
26–31	Job	ninth speech
32–37	Elihu	first and only speech
38–41	God	God speaks to Job
42	Job & God	Job repents & conclusion

Jehovah ('the LORD') is used at the beginning and the end of the book and in 12:9 to emphasize Job's dependence on the one true God (1:21; 38:1; 40:1, 3, 6; 42:1, 7, 9–11). Though Job was not an Israelite, he believed the evidence for the existence of the one true God in creation and the human conscience, and it appears he heard God's word to him personally (32:12). From Job 3 onwards three other names are used for God: *Eloah*, the singular of *Elohim*, translated 'God'; *Adoni* (28:28), normally 'Lord' in English translations; and *Shaddai*, 'the Almighty'. It is evident that all those mentioned in the book believed that God is to be feared and obeyed: 'Receive, please, instruction from His mouth, and lay up His words in your heart' (Eliphaz, 22:22); 'I have not departed from the commandment of His lips; I have treasured the words of His mouth more than my necessary food' (Job, 23:12).

1. What is the evidence for Job living c.2000 BC?
2. What do the names of God in this book reveal about the nature and being of God?
3. What other names are given to God in the Old Testament?
4. What titles are used to describe God's relationship with his people?

TO THINK ABOUT AND DISCUSS

1. Why is the Book of Job and Job himself so interesting?
2. Discuss how the names of God relate to the people of God.

1 Job's story

(1:1–22)

Life is always changing, and in Job 1 we have the history of the events that changed the lives of one man and his family for ever. These unexpected changes were unpleasant and painful—none more so than the sudden death of all of Job's children.

The problem of suffering is very real and our minds are focused on it when death confronts us. In the narrative, we find Job suffering from shock after multiple unforeseen bereavements. These wounds changed him for ever and numbed his soul in the short term. Yet Job was able to keep his faith and learn more clearly and profoundly about God's character and God's right to be feared, respected and obeyed.

Job's background (vv. 1–5)

Job was a godly man with a godly way of life. He feared God and shunned evil (1:8b)—that is, he possessed a reverential respect for God, having turned away from a life lived without God. In 2:3 God calls him 'blameless and upright'. Job was holy in God's eyes, having been cleansed from his sins. He was wholly fixed on the things of God through consecration and was full of love for God through sanctification. Like Noah, he found grace in the eyes of the Lord (Gen. 6:8). So Job was respected in heaven as well as on earth. Thus the opening chapters of the Book of Job make it clear that Job's sufferings were 'innocent' sufferings and his trials were not punishments from God because of law-breaking or disobedience (v. 8).

Job possessed great wealth, was of high social standing and was regarded as the greatest man of his generation (v. 3). He had 7,000 sheep, 3,000 camels, 500 yoke of oxen, 500 female donkeys and a large household consisting of seven sons, three daughters and many servants. This inventory of his assets is given to us, firstly, to secure Job as a real historical figure (see also Ezek. 14:14; James 5:11) and, secondly, to show that wealth is no protection from sorrows. In addition, the inventory emphasizes Job's righteousness, for he did not abuse his position of power and privilege.

It is also clear that Job was a man who possessed the light of life, for he knew that the way of salvation is by substitutionary penal atoning sacrifice. He offered burnt offerings on a regular basis for his sinful children (v. 5) because he knew about the sinfulness of sin in God's sight and that without the shedding of blood there is no forgiveness. Knowing the need for every individual soul to be personally forgiven, he made sure that offerings were made for *all* his children: 'according to the number of them all' (v. 5). This does not militate against an early date for the book. Abel, the son of Adam and Eve, knew to offer a blood atoning sacrifice to God in the earliest days of the world (Gen. 4:4). The need for every individual soul to be personally forgiven if peace with God is to be known still applies today. Thus we must all, by faith, make Jesus Christ our 'burnt offering' to God as a sacrifice for our sins and unbelief (Eph. 5:2).

Job's faithfulness (vv. 4–5)

Job possessed a deep love for his children and therefore properly set before them God's way of salvation. This responsibility is one that all parents have before God. They must not be satisfied with providing a good and healthy diet, a thorough education, the latest consumer goods or holidays abroad, or leaving them with a good inheritance in money, property or land. Job had riches, but he was also wise and spiritual. Parents must bring their children up to know Jesus Christ as their Saviour and Lord. This should be their greatest priority as guardians, because our offspring belong to God first by right of creation and then by right of redemption, through personal repentance and faith in Christ. If children fail to speak well of God and Jesus Christ his Son and his gospel, perhaps it is because their parents have failed in this most important matter of all. Most parents want the best for their children and will do what is right for them in every way they can. This is what God wants too, and it is what is expected of every father and mother.

According to the Bible, family life consists of one father, one mother and their children. This goes back to the Book of Genesis, where we read that God gave Adam a wife whom he called Eve. They were commanded to 'Be fruitful and multiply' (Gen. 1:28). Within the family unit, children are to 'obey [their] parents in all things, for this is well pleasing to the Lord' (Col. 3:20; see Exod. 20:12). Precious offspring must be instructed in what is right and what is wrong so that they will become good citizens and know God through his Son, Jesus Christ. Their attendance at Lord's Day worship, Sunday school and mid-week clubs will aid this process. When those children reach the age of majority they will make their own decisions and be responsible for their own actions and destiny (Prov. 22:6; Acts 5:29).

> Precious offspring must be instructed in what is right and what is wrong so that they will become good citizens and know God through his Son, Jesus Christ.

Job's faith (vv. 20–23)

In spite of the things that befell Job, his faith remained strong. Here we find Job's instinctive spiritual response to his tragic loss. What true grace Job showed when he 'arose, tore his robe, and shaved his head', then 'fell to the ground and worshiped' (v. 20). He accepted God's mysterious hand of providence for him and his wife and he retained the desire to worship and believe. Matthew Henry notes that weeping must not hinder worshipping.[1] This story of Job's suffering raises commonly asked questions about death, but what is clear at this juncture in the narrative is that Job accepted that the Lord (Jehovah) was in control over all circumstances, even death: 'Naked I came from my mother's womb, and naked shall I return there. The LORD gave, and the LORD has taken away; blessed be the name of the LORD' (v. 21).

Charles H. Spurgeon comments,

Sorrow can be greatly alleviated if we give serious thought to the Word. Evidently, this is what Job did when he said, 'Naked I came from my mother's womb, and naked shall I return there. The Lord gave, and the Lord has taken away; blessed be the name of the Lord' (1:21). Use Job as your example. Do not merely sit still and say 'I shall be comforted.' Look for themes on which to meditate profitably. Get an anchor-hold on some great and clearly ascertained truth, a truth in which you can have no possible doubt. Then you may begin to be comforted. When you have learned this lesson, you will have learned the art of comforting others.[2]

Because his faith was strong ...

Job acknowledged God as the Creator of all things

His faith told him that God had created Adam from the dust and Eve from Adam's side, and that this universe is God's handiwork (compare 9:8; 31:33; 33:4–6; 38:4, 12–13a; Gen. 1:26–27; 2:7, 21–25; Ps. 19).[3] His later reference to 'the Bear, Orion, and the Pleiades' (9:9) speaks of the stars created by God during the creation week (Gen. 1:16), and he saw the animal kingdom as God's creation, for God alone gives them life (12:7–10). Job had no thoughts of evolution and millions of years of suffering and bloodshed before Adam, nor would he have believed that people evolved from single-cell amoebae—not because he was scientifically ignorant (we shall see that the knowledge possessed by Job and his friends was far greater than we might imagine), but because he trusted the revelation given to him by God. He had not come into life as a descendant of apes or as the offspring of the so-called evolved *Homo erectus* ('upright man'). Job was to learn his place in God's universe and that he was created for fellowship with God. He would also learn to walk by faith and not by sight (Hab. 2:4; Mark 11:22; Rom. 5:2; 2 Cor. 5:7).

Job recognized that God is eternal and holy

'Naked shall I return there' (v. 21). God is called 'the Almighty' throughout the Book of Job, and more so in Job than in the rest of Scripture put together.[4] Job believed that God is the same yesterday, today and for ever, while recognizing that, as children of the first man Adam, we are all fallen sinners guilty of transgressing God's laws, which leads to death (14:1–4; compare 15:14; 34:14–15). Thus Job's theology (and anthropology) is in tune with that of the rest of the Old Testament and does not contradict the New (Rom. 3:23; 1 Tim. 6:7). He believed in a historical fall into ruin resulting in human depravity and the inability of men and women to save themselves, and understood that death is God's penalty for sin (1:5; 10:9; compare 25:4; Gen. 3:3; Rom. 3:23a). During Job's ninth speech, as he reflects on a life lived before God, he refers to the transgression of Adam which is imputed to all his posterity (31:33). Not for him the coming errors of Pelagius, or Semi-Pelagianism.[5] He was a fundamentalist of the best sort!

Job's righteousness (vv. 21–22)

In a matter of moments Job's world had been turned upside

down and inside out. His family had been destroyed and his business life was in meltdown, but he did not take the name of the Lord God in vain. He did not blaspheme or curse God. Instead, when bereaved, Job blessed his Saviour God without reserve. Later, it is true, he asks frank and honest questions—but without questions there can be no answers. In blessing God, Job showed that he was righteous and fully resigned to God's holy will for his life. He did not fight with God or accuse God of wickedness, as so many are inclined to do when bereaved of loved ones. When Job reached rock bottom he could do nothing other than rest on his God and Saviour's promises for his wife and himself.

This is the believer's best response to bereavement and pain. Falling back on the unchanging nature of God was the fruit of Job's regeneration and righteousness. All who face trials must do the same. Job never relinquished his faith in God. In fact, the paradox is that his faith became stronger, something that is always true when the people of God let sufferings draw them nearer to God in order to receive his grace in time of need (Rom. 8:28; Heb. 4:16). In the midst of grief, Jesus Christ offers peace instead of turmoil, strength in spite of weakness and hope for tomorrow (Matt. 11:28–30). Job had thought about suffering but, when it came, he was not prepared for the shock. In fact, he had always feared this tragedy which now befell him: 'For the thing I greatly feared has come upon me, and what I

> Falling back on the unchanging nature of God was the fruit of Job's regeneration and righteousness.

dreaded has happened to me. I am not at ease, nor am I quiet; I have no rest, for trouble comes' (3:25–26).

Emotional pain combined with physical pain was his lot at this time. Nevertheless, Job walked humbly and he accepted God's will. He did not blame God or charge him with evil (v. 22). Job's attitude was right and he was thinking clearly and biblically at this point. God had done no evil: 'The LORD gave, and the LORD has taken away; blessed be the name of the LORD' (v. 21b).

It is a common sin to impute unholy actions to the holy God and to be God's judge and jury. With a lack of fear and humility, people willingly pronounce a bitter and revengeful verdict on God and his actions. Job, as a righteous man possessing a God-given worldview, walked humbly before God. He feared God and shunned evil (v. 8b)—he possessed a reverential respect for God. His life matched his words and so he taught his children and servants by example. He was not hypocritical, nor was he fanatical in religion, but he held the spiritual ground between these two extremes. God says three times that Job was 'blameless and upright' (vv. 1, 8; 2:3) and we are told that 'Job feared God' (vv. 1, 9): this was a fear born of faith. His sufferings are therefore to be seen in the light of the sovereign providence of God and not because of his own sins. We are not saying, of course, that Job was without sin; that could not have been so (Rom. 3:10–18, 23); rather he was reckoned righteous in God's sight because of his faith.

Satan's attack was calculated not just to destroy Job's faith but also to expose (as Satan saw it) Job's hypocrisy: 'Does Job fear God for nothing? Have You not made a hedge around him, around his household, and around all that he has on every side? You have blessed the work of his hands, and his possessions have increased in the land. But now, stretch out Your hand and touch all that he has, and he will surely curse You to Your face!' (vv. 9–11). But he was wrong about Job; Satan cannot understand the work of saving grace in the souls of the redeemed, nor does he know what conversion is all about, it being a mystery to him. Instead, rather than curse God because of the sudden and unexpected loss of his ten lovely children and because of the shock of being robbed of all his great wealth, Job blessed God with sincerity: 'The LORD gave, and the LORD has taken away; blessed be the name of the LORD' (v. 21). It was Satan who was shocked and astonished! Although Job's sufferings fell within the sweep of God's sovereignty, it was Satan who was to be blamed for them.

Have you ever faced this kind of challenge? To respond to suffering as Job did is to keep faith and act righteously. Suffering can seem irrational and unfair. Job's sufferings did not make sense to him at first. They threatened both his understanding of God and his faith in God. They were so severe that Job wished that he had never been born (3:3). However, this was God's plan for his life:

Would he keep his faith? Would he keep praise on his lips? Would he keep the integrity he was now showing?

The story continues ...

FOR FURTHER STUDY

1. Job's view of creation is similar to that found in the account in Genesis 1–3. What is that account, and how can Christians be sure this account is accurate?

2. What are the proofs that Job was a real person living in the land of Uz?

3. What does the Bible mean when it tells us to resist the devil? Study Ephesians 4:27; 6:10–17; James 4:7.

TO THINK ABOUT AND DISCUSS

1. Were Job's reactions to God's providences sincere?

2. What is required of us in order to find peace when sudden bereavement or disaster strikes us?

3. We can be sure that Job's children knew where their father's priorities lay. If you have children, can you say the same of them regarding your priorities?

4. If you were in Job's place, would God be commending you before Satan? If so, why? If not, why not?

5. How can we make our children aware of Satan's existence and power without upsetting and worrying them?

2 Job's enemy

(2:1–13)

Job 2 opens with a second heavenly scene: 'Again there was a day when the sons of God came to present themselves before the LORD, and Satan came also among them to present himself before the LORD' (v. 1).

The phrase 'the sons of God' (1:6; 2:1) can be understood to mean angelic or heavenly beings. The New Testament states or implies that angels are created beings (Col. 1:15–17; Heb. 1:6–7). In this chapter they meet with God, presenting themselves before him. Satan is with them because he too 'is the servant of God's purposes, being permitted to do his evil work in order to further the will of God'.[1] Does this meeting take place in heaven? To free us from the difficulty of thinking that a fallen and diabolical angelic enemy is allowed to enter heaven, some have suggested that 'there is another realm, another place, where God holds council with his heavenly court and where actions are taken which affect people on earth'.[2] However, no other venue has been revealed as a possible location. It is apparent that wherever this meeting takes place, God himself is perfectly at ease with the situation. Some think that the sons of God gathered to receive orders; the verb 'to present' (v. 1) could be translated 'to await orders'.

In 38:4–7 we find a clue as to when God created angels:

Where were you when I laid the foundations of the earth?

Tell Me, if you have understanding.

Who determined its measurements?

Surely you know!

Or who stretched the line upon it?

To what were its foundations fastened?

Or who laid its cornerstone,

When the morning stars sang together,

And all the sons of God shouted for joy?

The mention of 'morning stars' and 'the sons of God' indicates the presence of the angels at the birth of the universe.[3] Men and angels alone in God's creation can sing to the praise of God's glory.[4] This is something the ape primates cannot do as they are not so designed.

Satan's identity and ability (vv. 1–6)

Satan's identity

Angels are invisible and immortal but not immutable. When created, they were endowed with intellect, will and beauty, and power far above the human level. They all worshipped God in the excellence of holiness, until the fall of Satan. When created by God the angels were good. Some, however, fell from their celestial wisdom and position through the misuse of their liberty.[5]

Thus Satan was not created evil, but through pride and self-love fell from grace (Isa. 14:12–14). He is the adversary of the people of God, constantly accusing them day and night (1 Peter 5:8; Rev. 12:10). In the Bible, Satan is also given the following names:

- The devil—the slanderer (Matt. 4:1)
- Apollyon—the destroyer (Rev. 9:11)
- Beelzebub—the prince of demons (Matt. 12:24)

In this chapter we immediately find Satan's true character revealed, exposing his malice and cunning. He appears as a real being, and this fits with the testimony of the rest of Scripture (Gen. 3:4, 14; Zech. 3:1; Matt. 4:1–11; Jude 9). Created intelligent and powerful, he is always scheming against the people of God.

Satan's ability

Satan is the chief enemy of God's people, and the chief of all the powers that are opposed to them. The Bible describes him in various ways, such as:

- A roaring lion (1 Peter 5:8)
- A strong man (Luke 11:21)
- A dragon (Rev. 12:3–4)
- The prince of the power of the air (Eph. 2:2)
- The god of this age (2 Cor. 4:4)

In Ephesians Paul says that we must resist the devil; he is a force to be reckoned with. This resistance is achieved by Christians putting on the whole armour of God (Eph. 6:11), which enables believers to stand against the devil's schemes.

However, we are to be aware that he is not omnipresent nor omniscient. He knows the past but not the future, and is limited by God in his attributes and actions. His works are indeed evil in the extreme, and he uses the minds of men and women, intending always to create discord and conflict among the people of God, while doing his best as a 'roaring lion' to deceive and destroy those created in God's image (1 Peter 5:8). He must, however, obey God and yield to him; he cannot do anything without God's permission (Job 1:12; 2:4–6). His immense power includes the ability to stir up whole tribes of people to steal, kill and murder. Job's livestock was stolen by the Sabeans, his camels were raided by the Chaldeans, and the same tribe murdered some of his servants in the skirmish (1:17). His sheep and servants were consumed by fire that fell from heaven (lightning?) and his ten children were killed by a violent storm (1:16, 19). Job knew nothing of the meeting in heaven. He was unaware of the activities behind the scene and the arrangement between God and Satan. He knew only that what he had feared had come to pass (3:25).

God's plan (vv. 3–6)

> Then the LORD said to Satan, 'Have you considered My servant Job, that there is none like him on the earth, a blameless and upright man, one who fears God and shuns evil? And still he holds fast to his integrity, although you incited Me against him, to destroy him without cause.'

v. 3

God tells Satan that Job is a saved man, but Satan does not believe in the power of the grace of God to transform the human heart and wants another opportunity to prove *his* theory that all sinners are hypocrites (vv. 4–5). Satan understands fallen human nature, but not the new nature born of faith (1 Peter 1:23). God allows this next test to take place in order for Job to bear witness, through suffering, to the power of true conversion: 'And the LORD said to Satan, "Behold, he is in your hand, but spare his life"' (v. 6).

Job overcomes Satan because of 'the power of God through faith' (1 Peter 1:5; Jude 24). God is always one step ahead of Satan. The evil one must give way to the Holy One (Job 1:12; 2:6). Job was chosen out of this world and made the special object of divine affection. He is regarded by God as a 'blameless and upright man, one who fears God and shuns evil ... And still he holds fast to his integrity' (2:3). This is God's declaration that Job is righteous. In gospel terms, Job is a man who has been justified by faith (Rom. 5:1) and is 'right with God'. Here is one in whom Christ dwells by his Spirit. He has Christ's righteousness imputed to him by faith and he possesses an inner strength born of that same faith, giving a sure ground for hope.

Satan's second attack (vv. 7–8)

Satan does not give up easily, nor does he show mercy to Job; and he treats all God's people likewise. It is his nature to do so as he is fallen and wicked; as the Bible says, the leopard cannot 'change ... its spots' (Jer. 13:23), and neither can Satan. He moves against Job unjustly, without a cause: 'So Satan went out from the presence of the LORD, and struck Job with painful boils from the sole of his foot to the crown of his head. And he took for himself a potsherd with which to scrape himself while he sat in the midst of the ashes' (vv. 7–8).

God's acceptance of Satan's challenge to test Job's loyalty and love was intended to show the power of his saving grace. Why is Satan so mixed up about this? He is intelligent, and has a grasp of history second to none. He knows that the fallen heart is lustful and self-centred (v. 4). However, he

> God's acceptance of Satan's challenge to test Job's loyalty and love was intended to show the power of his saving grace.

cannot fathom the mystery of sovereign, unwarranted grace. We see that this is not only Satan's problem, but it belongs to the good angels too. They are somewhat perplexed about the gospel message, having the 'desire to look into' these things (1 Peter 1:12).

Job's righteous response (v. 10)

> Shall we indeed accept good from God, and shall we not accept adversity?

These famous words are once again proof of Job's faith in a benevolent sovereign Creator. All the suffering, pain and disease in the world are due to what the Bible calls the fall into sin (Gen. 3). Paul mentions this historic, real event in Romans 5, affirming that if there had been no fall in the Garden of Eden, there would be no need for a Saviour. There are some things we just cannot explain unless we take into account that this is the genesis of all suffering and death in the world (Rom. 8:21–22).

Job reacted to Satan's blows as if he had known

2 Corinthians 4:16–17: '… we do not lose heart. Even though our outward man is perishing, yet the inward man is being renewed day by day. For our light affliction, which is but for a moment, is working for us a far more exceeding and eternal weight of glory.' Job's faith told him that God is good. Nevertheless, as we shall see, his experiences raised the question 'Why?' in his heart.

The apostle James helps us to understand God's dealings with his fallen and redeemed people. In his epistle we read, 'Indeed we count them blessed who endure. You have heard of the perseverance of Job and seen the end intended by the Lord—that the Lord is very compassionate and merciful' (5:11). The apostle holds up Job as a good example of true faith, patience and determined perseverance while under trial. Job was not quitting; he believed that God is good. Yet James implies that the whole incident was about the revealing of God's character: 'that the Lord is very compassionate and merciful'. Satan's attacks were nasty and wicked, Job's trials were long and miserable, but God meant it all for good. Job was able to accept this. 'Shall we indeed accept good from God, and shall we not accept adversity?' (v. 10).

Job's wife (vv. 9–10a)

> Then his wife said to him, 'Do you still hold fast to your integrity? Curse God and die!' But he said to her, 'You speak as one of the foolish women speaks.'

Job's wife appeared to think that he was blindly refusing to face the reality of his desperate situation. Did she feel that God had abandoned him? That is a common reaction when

God's people go through illness and very difficult times, but it was not the case with Job.

If Job's wife was, as it seems, trying to urge him to renounce his faith, this would have been an extra, fourth, trial. However, this was absolutely the time to stick together in order that they might comfort and support each other, for 'Two are better than one' (Eccles. 4:9). She may have been speaking thus through the shock and the bitterness of bereavement and because she felt that her husband was suffering unjustly. Was she doped by the drug of emotional pain? Did these things drive her to say, in effect, 'You are a good man and you do not deserve what God has done to you: you do not deserve such treatment'? If so, she would not be alone in feeling this way when bereavement breaks the heart, numbs the mind and pains the soul. If, on the other hand, Job's wife was angry with God, again this is not an uncommon reaction to the loss of those who are very close to us. However, it is evident that she could not understand why Job was not angry too. She could not keep her feelings in, but 'In all this Job did not sin with his lips' (v. 10).

Job recognized that both goodness and trouble come from God. Thus he anticipated one of the central messages of the Book of Job, which is that the Divine Will is sovereign. If we love God, we will trust him. This is not a work of the flesh, but the fruit of a renewed heart born of God's Spirit (John 3:3). There is need for today's generation to let God be God! He needs to be seen as the *Westminster Shorter Catechism* describes him: 'God is a Spirit, infinite, eternal, and unchangeable, in his being, wisdom, power, holiness, justice, goodness, and truth.'[6] We all need to accept that he is Lord of creation, providence and salvation. God will do what he wants to do and when it suits him. How sad when sinful men and women argue that they must be free to exercise their own (fallen) wills as they see fit, and then deny God the same right! Job had no such idea, for he was already enlightened and, through his sufferings, would gain fuller and clearer knowledge of his Redeemer. The psalmist says, 'Trust in Him at all times' (Ps. 62:8). Job was learning this important lesson. God is the judge of all right and wrong, and of all hearts and minds.

FOR FURTHER STUDY

1. What is righteousness, according to the Bible? Give Bible references to back up your explanation.

2. What is it that Satan cannot do?

3. Find out more about the distinction between God's perfect will and his permissive will.

4. What tactics did Satan use to try to destroy Job's faith (2 Cor. 2:11)?

TO THINK ABOUT AND DISCUSS

1. How do you respond to Job's wife's comment in 2:9?

2. James the brother of John was killed in a time of persecution, not long after Pentecost, by King Herod (Acts 12:2), yet God made sure that Satan did not kill Job. Can we understand why God allowed one and not the other?

3. Job said, 'Shall we indeed accept good from God, and shall we not accept adversity?' How can we hold this same attitude when we go through difficult times?

4. Read Romans 8:28–31. What are its implications in the context of human suffering?

3 Job's lament

(3:1–26)

In their discourses, Job and his friends discuss the problems of human existence in a fallen universe. Job's friends and family (42:11) interpret his condition as the result of gross sin when they see him sitting on the town's ash heap outside the city gate (2:8; see 42:11). The wisdom of the day is unable to cope with Job's needs and he is found bankrupt.

However, through the course of his trials and his debates with his three friends, Job learned lessons that God's people must always be learning and relearning. Believing in and trusting in the greatness and goodness of God was a major help for Job and he found peace when he let God be God. He learned to hope in the God of hope (Rom. 15:13). Our finite minds are not able to see the big picture, so understanding all the ways of God escapes us. Job, though, learned not to lean on his own understanding of things but rather to trust God at all times (Prov. 3:5–6).

Job's search for peace

Job has sat for seven days in silence surrounded by his friends Eliphaz the Temanite, Bildad the Shuhite and Zophar the Naamathite (2:11–13). They are in sympathy with Job's pain and stay with him to let him know that he is not alone. This, however, is not enough to help Job, as we shall see.

Job now speaks in the bitterness of his soul: 'Job ... cursed the day of his birth' (v. 1). The Hebrew word translated 'cursed' and meaning 'to hold in contempt' is elsewhere employed of cursing God (Exod. 22:28; Lev. 24:15) or one's parents (Exod. 21:17). The feelings and attitudes we find here are shared by many who have had similar experiences to those of Job. His great losses take a toll on his attitude, which now flows from the old sinful nature, and he begins to declare its feelings. Yes, he is still righteous in God's eyes; he is still a redeemed person; but now he seeks answers, feeling offended by his personal calamities—it is the 'perfect storm' for him to endure. However, Job does not commit blasphemy. He does not seek revenge, neither does he express thoughts of suicide. As a man who walks with God, Job is righteous, but as a sinner (saved by grace) living in a fallen world, he is still prone to the fears and cares of everyday life, especially when they centre on his children and business life. His anxiety is shared by millions of believers around the world when in similar circumstances. He expresses a sense of horror and inner anguish, as doubly emphasized by the synonyms 'fear' and 'dread': 'For the thing I greatly feared has come upon me, and what I dreaded has happened to me. I am not at ease, nor am I quiet; I have no rest, for trouble comes' (vv. 25–26).

It is evident that Job has no peace of heart and his mind is in turmoil, searching for answers. His problem, one shared by many, is why did God allow this to happen? He looks for peace and closure. As we will see, peace of heart and mind is found only in the acceptance of God's will and the way he deals with his adopted children. This process brings strength for today and hope for tomorrow through our risen Saviour Jesus Christ.

Bitterness and anger

Job later admits to being bitter because of his condition and losses (7:11; 9:18). This increases his sufferings, injures his soul and sours his heart. Bitterness means holding a resentful spirit that refuses reconciliation. Our fallen human natures often respond in resentment when we are neglected, hurt or offended. This can create a reservoir of hatred in the soul that will break fellowship with others and lead to personal backsliding. Its effects are a loss of joy, an increase in criticism, a lack of prayer and a hardening of the heart. Anger is another strong emotion provoked by bereavement and it is often linked with the question 'Why?' or 'Why me?' Times of suffering cause us to seek answers from experts such as medical staff, police, doctors, the clergy or family members. Anger can be directed towards a person or an event and even towards God himself, as we find in the Book of Job. A sense of injustice or futility may grip the mind, resulting in anger which questions God's purposes and love and is tempted to reject his help. Anger, rage, evil-speaking and malice are all fruits of bitterness (Eph. 4:31). Bitterness likes to justify its sourness by claiming to be right and accusing others of wrong. However, bitterness is a putrefying bog that will swallow up all the kindness and friendship once shown to others (Heb. 12:15). It will make one retreat from others, refuse reconciliation and be rendered redundant in divine service. Bitterness must be dealt with by repentance; bitterness unrepented of will potentially destroy the spiritual life in a professing believer and can lead to murder (Mark 6:19), wreck a local church and even shake a fist in the face of God. The forgiveness of others is the antidote to the poison of bitterness (Matt. 6:14–15; Eph. 4:32).

Job's way of peace

There are times in life when we feel trapped. Job now feels this way because he has more questions on his mind than answers received from God. It is as if he is the prisoner of God's providence and will. He sees himself as hedged in and unable to escape: 'For the thing I greatly feared has come upon me, and what I dreaded has happened to me' (v. 25). He sighs and groans (literally 'roars', v. 24), thereby expressing his frustration and impatience with his plight. In this state of heart he begins to search for the answers he longs for.

Full of anxiety, fretting and disquiet, Job wants an explanation! We can call his enquiry 'The Big Why'—that is, why suffering? We will look at this in more detail in the next chapter, but one answer for now is that suffering awakens the sluggish soul to God. God can take failure and turn it into success. Suffering gives us the opportunity to turn to God for help; the alternative is to turn against God. In other words, suffering either humbles us or hardens us. If we are angry with God, perhaps we need to stop fighting and trust him for peace, grace and new hope through his Son, Jesus Christ (John 14:1, 27). Job is struggling with this: 'I am not at ease, nor am I quiet; I have no rest, for trouble comes' (v. 26). He has no inner peace at this time. He needs help. It is only faith and trust such as Job expressed before (1:21) that gives to the soul the peace of God that passes all understanding. This kind of peace was commended by Paul to the Philippians (Phil. 4:6–7).

A biblical response to suffering

What should be faith's response to life's tragedies? The comfort of God's peace is found by accepting Jesus Christ's strength given to us in the gospel. Saving faith offers new life and divine strength to carry on. Jesus said, 'My grace is sufficient for you, for My strength is made perfect in weakness' (2 Cor. 12:9). Again, in John's Gospel we hear the call to believe and receive: 'Peace I leave with you, My peace I give to you; not as the world gives do I give to you. Let not your heart be troubled, neither let it be afraid' (John 14:27).

> The peace that Christ gives banishes fear and dread from the heart, for Jesus is in control of all circumstances.

The peace that Christ gives banishes fear and dread from the heart, for Jesus is in control of all circumstances (Col. 1:16). Christ's peace in the face of bereavement can be known if faith turns to trust, and trust rests on the promises of God in Jesus Christ. This comfort experienced in fellowship with the Holy Spirit is powerful, lasting and consoling. Progress in grace and in the knowledge of Christ is part of the warp and woof of Christian experience. Charles H. Spurgeon says,

> Trials do not come by chance (1 Peter 1:6–7). Trials are sent because God judges them necessary (James 1:12). Trials are weighed out with discretion and are given by cautious wisdom. 'Trials' is a beautiful name for affliction. I do not look on affliction as a judgment for my sins, for my sin has been punished in Christ (1 Peter 2:24). Rather, I look on my affliction as coming from the all-wise judgment of a kind and infinitely wise Father. Afflictions are called judgments not because they are judicial but because they are judicious.[1]

These beautiful but fiery trials work *for* us, 'being much more precious than gold', for by them God is refining and perfecting us in order that we will bring him 'praise, honor, and glory at the revelation of Jesus Christ' (1 Peter 1:7). Job was not forsaken by the Lord, but he *was* struck down for a while. The Lord spared his life so that he could continue to testify to God's deliverance and grace, while learning how truly gracious and longsuffering God really is.

We should think through our theology of suffering so that we may be a little more prepared for 'the treadmill of pain' when it comes. It appears that Job was not prepared for the shock, but we cannot blame him. All seemed well with his children and his finances, but they were taken from him when the hand of providence struck. Such is the shock and pain of bereavement; it is like jumping into a cold lake. The people of God may think about it, but it is not until they are immersed in its icy waters that they feel its shock. For Job, it seemed so irrational and unfair that it left him thoroughly perplexed.

During times like this, faith in God and in Jesus Christ is threatened. Would Job pull away and be bitter towards his Maker and drift into unbelief? Would he disown God, thinking of him as a figment of the imagination and the trick of a deceived religious mind, or would he humble himself and accept good and evil from God's hand? Job's contact with the 'perfect storm' was so severe that he wished he had never been born: 'For now I would have lain still and been quiet, I would have been asleep; then I would have been at rest' (v. 13). The unexpected and the unwanted had become the reality and Job asked frank and honest questions. But what he went through was to be interpreted in the belief that God is love: 'the Lord is very compassionate and merciful' (James 5:11). This foundation will steer readers and students of the Scriptures away from the paths of unbelief and scepticism. These paths are all around us and were described in John Bunyan's *The Pilgrim's Progress* as 'By-path Meadow'.[2] The people of God are not to doubt his goodness in the land of the living. Every promise of God is theirs in Christ Jesus (2 Cor. 1:20).

Job's speeches reveal his understanding of divine revelation through nature (see Ps. 19) and his right standing before God. He asks questions and approaches God boldly, gaining that access that believers have in Christ before the throne of grace (Heb. 4:16). His questions are candid, yet God does not condemn this, but rather responds with grace and firmness. Job comes to his Father in heaven, trusting that his humble faith will keep him on the straight and narrow (2:10). When bereavement, pain and dark providences are upon the people of God, they must do the same, believing that he will carry them through.

In times like these you need a Saviour;

In times like these you need an anchor;

Be very sure, be very sure

Your anchor holds and grips the Solid Rock![3]

For further study ▶

FOR FURTHER STUDY

1. What other portions of the Bible are especially helpful in developing a biblical response to suffering?

2. What attributes of God help us to cope when death and pain enter our lives?

3. What is the Christian answer to the affliction of bitterness?

4. Reflect on 2 Corinthians 1:20. What promises are meant in this verse?

TO THINK ABOUT AND DISCUSS

1. How do you tend to respond when afflicted by trials? How does your response match up with a biblical response, and how can you be prepared to respond biblically during future trials?

2. How can others help the bereaved (2 Cor. 1:3–7)?

3. Why was it that Job, after appearing to be meek before God, appears aggressive and bitter in the chapters following?

4 Job's grief

(4:1–7:21)

Eliphaz is the first of Job's friends to take the opportunity to speak (chs 4–5). Job had already been suffering for some time before Eliphaz arrived to help.

I f we remember that communication was a great deal slower in Job's day than today, and that his three friends had made special arrangements to travel together before they arrived to be with Job (2:11), it is possible that some months had elapsed by the time they reached him. This would then be what is meant by Job's words in 7:3: 'So I have been allotted months of futility, and wearisome nights have been appointed to me.' Job cannot see any meaning in his predicament. He is utterly puzzled by it and has no peace of heart or mind. He is left with many questions and a search for the truth.

Eliphaz commends Job for the help he has given to others in the past (4:3–4) but soon puts in the proverbial knife and says that Job has changed his tune now that *he* is on the receiving end of misfortune! Eliphaz sees all suffering as punishment for sin and misconduct; therefore Job, who is now in the midst of suffering, must be guilty of crimes before God. His two companions share this theology and are therefore not able to help Job in his search for truth and peace. However, it was part of God's plan that these three friends were at Job's side to engage him in dialogue so that he would find out more about the nature of God and his dealings with his people during their earthly pilgrimage.

Eliphaz comes across as opinionated and self-taught (see, for example, his references to his dream in 4:12–16). He becomes exasperated, harsh and bitter in his accusations during his later speeches. It is evident that Eliphaz and the two other companions have not grasped the big picture and lack awareness of the work of God's grace in perfecting the soul. Job, however, is searching to understand the ways of the heavenly Father with his adopted children.

Biblical reasons for suffering

Job answers Eliphaz with a question of his own: 'Have I sinned?' (7:20). Job is not perfect, neither does he think that he is, but Eliphaz is not right to think that all suffering is the result of personal guilt. However, the object of Job's anger is not Eliphaz but God: 'Have I sinned? What have I done to You, O watcher of men? Why have You set me as Your target, so that I am a burden to myself?' (7:20).

He cannot understand why he is subject to an apparently gratuitous hostile attack from God, who sees all things, knows all things, and reads the hearts of all people. His retort is, in effect, saying, 'Why me, Lord?' because disappointment, disease, difficulties and dark providences are a challenge to his understanding of the God of creation. There are valid biblical reasons for suffering. For example, if Paul had not been imprisoned, we would not be in possession of the prison epistles of the New Testament (Philippians, Colossians, Ephesians and Philemon). If John Bunyan had not spent years in Bedford jail, his great masterpiece, *The Pilgrim's Progress*, would never have been written. Some see no purpose in suffering. However, the Book of Job helps with answers to this problem if we will receive them. What are the causes of illness according to God's Word? We will look at four possibilities here.

The fall into sin

Suffering, disease and death are the result of Adam's first sin in the Garden of Eden (Rom. 5:12). The fall into sin is recorded for us in Genesis 3 as a historical event, as is also proved by the New Testament writers. All pain, disease and death find their origin here. There is no evidence in the Bible that there was death and bloodshed before the fall; rather God saw that everything before the fall was 'very good' (Gen. 1:31). When Adam sinned, the whole of creation fell and his failure brought death and suffering to the whole universe (Rom. 8:18–21). Nature is 'red in tooth and claw'[1] because of Adam's first sin. There are some consequences of the fall which will not be changed or rectified until eternity. Although we are puzzled when bad things happen to good people, we are called to trust God; and although bad health can often be linked to a poor diet, a lack of exercise and a bad environment, the Bible tells us that ultimately our lifespan is in God's loving hands (Ps. 31:15).

Satan

We must not forget about Satan. He is clearly implicated in Job's grief and sufferings (2:7) and is also, therefore, the cause of much suffering in this world. The Book of Job is not alone in attributing sickness and disaster to the devil. The New Testament gives other examples of Satan's power to afflict people's bodies (Luke 13:16; Acts 10:38; 2 Cor. 12:7). Satan can, with God's permission, do harm and cause sorrow and suffering among the human race, but he is not able to destroy the grace of God in the redeemed.

It appears that this satanic curse affected Job's whole body, 'from the sole of his foot to the crown of his head' (2:7). The physical signs were painful boils (sores full of pus), which were infected with worms (7:5) and were relieved somewhat by scraping the flesh; difficulty in movement (2:7–8); disfiguration (2:12); bad breath (19:17); much pain (30:17); and darkening and shrivelling of the skin (30:30). It is right to suppose that this affliction was designed by Satan to be as painful and untreatable as possible without being terminal. Satan wanted the testing of Job to come out in his favour, so he did his evil best to achieve this. The lack of a clearer description of Job's symptoms means that we cannot determine which disease afflicted Job. It is possible that he was suffering from several chronic diseases at once.

Personal sinfulness

Errors of judgement, wrong choices or wilful disobedience that transgresses God's commands can also be the cause of illness. Sickness can be brought on by a lack of good hygiene, exercise and good diet. Gluttony and the excessive use of alcohol, drugs and tobacco have been clinically shown to cause health problems. Some Scriptures indicate that sickness and sins go hand-in-hand (Matt. 9:2; John 5:14; 1 Cor. 11:30).

This, however, is *not* why Job is suffering. We can be sure about this, for God makes it clear (1:8; 2:3). This in turn allows us to recognize that Job's friends are wrong in insinuating that he is being punished by God as a result of his unrighteousness. Professor Fred Leahy says, 'There is sickness where there is no sin but it is accountable only to the sovereignty and grace of God.'[2] It is to be remembered that Jesus Christ said that sickness and personal calamity are not always caused by sin: 'Neither this man nor his parents sinned, but that the works of God should be revealed in him' (John 9:3). The man spoken of had been blind from birth, but it was neither his fault nor his parents'. Here again we see the dealings of a sovereign God. God does indeed sometimes use sickness punitively. This is seen in the case of Moses (Exod. 4:24); Miriam (Num. 12:10); and Elymas the sorcerer, who was struck blind for opposing the gospel (Acts 13:8). Because of King David's sin with Bathsheba, the sword never departed from his house (2 Sam. 12:10).

> It is to be remembered that Jesus Christ said that sickness and personal calamity are not always caused by sin.

Our sanctification

Our theology of suffering needs to take into account God's

way of sanctifying his redeemed people. God deals with his people like 'a refiner and a purifier of silver' (Mal. 3:3), in a fatherly way correcting them for their own eternal good. In Job 5:17 Eliphaz brings up the issue of correction through chastening by God. This is a recurring theme in the Bible and is relevant to Job (Prov. 3:11–12; Rev. 3:19). The Book of Job shows that suffering can lead to a clearer and profounder vision of God: 'I have heard of You by the hearing of the ear, but now my eye sees You. Therefore I abhor myself, and repent in dust and ashes' (42:5–6). The Epistle to the Hebrews reveals that chastening leads to holiness in those who cooperate with God: He 'chastened us … that we may be partakers of His holiness' (Heb. 12:10).

God's hand of correction on his saints is to be looked on as a blessing, a birthright and the privilege of sonship. During times of suffering, the heart must keep pace with the mind and our affections with the intellect. The psalmist, when perplexed, said, 'Unite my heart to fear Your name' (Ps. 86:11). This is because in Hebrew the 'heart' included the affections, the will and the mind. All three are represented in the soul's inner spiritual life. The psalmist prays for them to agree and to be as one; until they are, he cannot praise the Lord his God wholeheartedly (v. 12). Our minds may tell us that God is good and does only good, but do we love him with all our hearts? Our minds tell us that we should keep the laws of God, but do our wills always agree? The psalmist's prayer should be ours. The agreement of heart, mind and will is achieved by the work of the Holy Spirit. He works to produce meekness in us, and he allows us to see the big picture while drawing our affections after Jesus

Christ our Saviour. There is a need for us to remember that 'He who has begun a good work in you will complete it until the day of Jesus Christ' (Phil. 1:6). In 2 Corinthians 12:7 we read these words of Paul: 'Lest I should be exalted above measure by the abundance of revelations, a thorn in the flesh was given to me ... to buffet me.' Three times Paul asked to be free of the pain, but God said kindly, 'My grace is sufficient for you' (v. 9). We are meant to humble ourselves in response to God's providential care of us (1 Peter 5:6–7). So we can say that suffering is sometimes given to prevent further sinfulness on the believer's part.

The New Testament assures God's people that suffering is not worthless nor needless (Rom. 5:3–4; 8:28–30). Job was in need of biblical hope and was to learn to look to God alone for it. To miss the blessing suffering affords (because it casts the soul on Jesus) is to be left without hope. In the light of eternity our sufferings will prove to have been good for us as God's agents of reproof, correction and discipline (Heb. 12). Suffering has brought the church great books and hymns, and great saints.

The question 'Why me?' is often on the lips of God's people. However, it should really be, 'Why not me?', a more humble response to personal suffering. 'What have I done to deserve this?' is another lament that comes to our lips when in trouble. It is our response to suffering that is important, and Job helps us to react well to it. Robert Murray M'Cheyne understood this:

Learn the certainty of sanctification. Rutherford said, 'Blessed be God, Christ is a whole Saviour—He not only justifies but he sanctifies too.' Oh, no, he will not lose the end for which he died—to make you not of this world, while you are in the world. He came to this miserable world, and took stones to polish for His Father's palace. Do you ever think He will leave you unholy? This is the will of the Father, even your sanctification. Jesus died, and the Spirit is sent as a sanctifier. There is much sin between you and God—many temptations—yet you shall be made holy (Eph. 2:10; 1 Thes. 5:23).[3]

FOR FURTHER STUDY

1. Why is there need for sanctification in the people of God?
2. What is the role of patience and faith in suffering? Back up your answer with Scripture references.
3. How can we make sure that heart, mind and will are harmonized when it comes to the will of God our Saviour (Ps. 86)?

TO THINK ABOUT AND DISCUSS

1. How does God use suffering positively in our lives (see 2 Cor. 1:3–8; 12:7)? Have you seen suffering produce positive effects in your own life, or in the lives of others?
2. According to God's Word, are there other causes of illness than those stated above?
3. How should we deal with personal sin and guilt?

5 Job's prayer

(8:1–10:22)

Bildad's first speech in Job 8 reveals his lack of wisdom and sympathy. He makes hurtful accusations when addressing Job. He ties the violent death of Job's ten children to their sins and insinuates that they got what they deserved (v. 4)!

This is not what a bereaved person, in a time of immense sorrow, needs to hear. There is no justification from the text for this idea. Yes, Job's children were sinners, as are we all (Rom. 3:23), but the Book of Job does not conclude that that was why they died. If Scripture is silent on this matter, then we must be also.

The words 'pure and upright' (8:6) describe that quality of character of heart and mind the new birth produces, but Bildad, not having a clear understanding of the work of the Holy Spirit, cannot see that sinners saved by grace are still apt to sin. Like Eliphaz, Bildad sees everything in black and white. Therefore, he thinks Job must be suffering because of his own personal guilt. He cannot understand the doctrine of justification by faith alone. According to Bildad, Job is a hypocrite; he likens Job to a man who deserves what he is getting (8:13). Job is now accused of being an actor who pretends to be righteous and refuses to admit he has sins to confess, and who needs to acknowledge that God is dealing with him justly. His prosperity was short-lived because of his sins. In Bildad's mind, God does not cast out the 'blameless' or 'perfect'. Therefore, since Job has been cast out, he cannot have been blameless, but must have been guilty of offending God (8:20–22).

Here we see Bildad making Job's life a misery and adding to his many present sorrows by equating Job's sufferings with the just actions of a righteous God towards a deserving transgressor. He has passed judgement without any biblical evidence to support his conclusion. He has equated material blessings with the rewards of righteous living, just as the 'prosperity gospel' in our day has done. Yet it was God's view of Job that mattered, not what his three friends thought. So with us, the ultimate test is not what others think of us, but what God thinks.

Job's knowledge of God (9:1–35)

The holy God (vv. 1–3)

> Then Job answered and said:
> 'Truly I know it is so,
> But how can a man be righteous before God?
> If one wished to contend with Him,
> He could not answer Him one time out of a thousand.

Job's response to Bildad shows that he acknowledges the truth of some of what has been said. He knows that man cannot contend successfully with God (v. 3) and that he (Job) does speak out of turn at times (v. 20). He becomes more agitated and struggles as he grapples with his problems and the reasons for them. However, there is an important question on his heart: 'how can a man be righteous before God?' (v. 2). Job is asking about the need for a mediator (v. 33). However, the universality of suffering in this fallen world means that no one can escape its painful hand. In context, Job wonders what it will take for a person to be exempt from suffering; who can avoid it, if all are condemned by God? Although Job knows himself to be righteous (justified) in God's sight, he also knows that he could not defend himself in God's courts of justice (vv. 14–15). The innocent and the wicked alike experience disasters that engulf them (vv. 22–23). This perplexes Job. Job's pain and bewilderment continue to fill his soul with bitterness (v. 18b).

> The universality of suffering in this fallen world means that no one can escape its painful hand … The innocent and the wicked alike experience disasters that engulf them.

God the Creator (vv. 4–10)

Job knows a lot about God and his world. He is a godly man with a godly way of life, and God is the object of his faith and worship. Job possesses a faith in God that is hard to find today, expressed in verses 7–10:

He commands the sun, and it does not rise;

He seals off the stars;

He alone spreads out the heavens,

And treads on the waves of the sea;

He made the Bear, Orion, and the Pleiades,

And the chambers of the south;

He does great things past finding out,

Yes, wonders without number.

Is Job thinking of the biblical creation account of when the stars were created on the fourth day of the creation week (Gen. 1:16; compare Job 26:13)? It seems likely. His statement in verse 8—'He alone spreads out the heavens'—echoes the creation account words 'He made the stars also' (Gen. 1:16; Ps. 147:4). Here Job compares the height of heaven with the infinity of God (Job 11:7–8; 22:12). At the same time, he is happy to accept the uniformity of stellar positions and movements, as annually observed by the human eye for as long as people have gazed on them: 'He made the Bear, Orion, and the Pleiades' (v. 9). The stars 'are used to set the time, to determine the latitude and longitude, to establish directions and locations anywhere on earth for navigation and other uses that require extreme precision. They were in fact created "for signs and seasons, and for days and years"' (Gen. 1:14).[1] Not only were the stars created to be our guides, but we are very specifically told that they were made 'to give light on the earth' (Gen. 1:15, 17). This was to make a distinction between the ancient Near Eastern heathen idea that the stars were themselves gods to be feared and worshipped.[2]

God has grouped the stars in constellations: 'He made the Bear, Orion, and the Pleiades' (v. 9; see also 26:13; 38:31–33;

Ps. 19:1). The Bear (Arcturus) is seen in the summer sky (northern latitudes) and found in the Boötes constellation. It is a giant red star, larger than the sun, and the fourth brightest star in the earth's night sky which can also be seen during the day. The Orion constellation has three bright blue stars in a straight line which make up Orion's belt and which are instantly recognizable on a clear winter's night. The Pleiades is also known as the 'seven sisters' and is a cluster consisting of a few hundred stars, although only six or seven are visible to the naked eye. It lies in the constellation Taurus, the bull.[3] Job and his contemporaries would have been able to see around five thousand stars which are visible at night. Today, 'Astronomers now estimate, however, that there are more than 400 billion stars in the Milky Way galaxy, and that there are 125 billion galaxies in the universe. The total number of stars is estimated at 1×10 to the power 22, or 10 billion trillions. Moreover, the God who created all of these, the Holy One of Israel, even calls them all by name and ensures that "not one is missing".'[4]

God the Saviour (vv. 11–35)

Job now begins to realize that part of the solution to his quest is found in knowing himself as God knows him, and this makes him feel bad: 'I am blameless, yet I do not know myself; I despise my life' (v. 21).

Trouble brings out the best or the worst in people. Job's character is being shaped for the better through his trials and troubles (Ps. 138:8; Phil. 1:6). Is there patience, humility and hope, or is there anger, bitterness and unbelief still to be uprooted in the heart? Job is learning about himself. We all need to know ourselves and how to handle ourselves in times of trial and pain. Most of all, Job sees his personal need of a mediator, believing that only such a person will be able to help him (v. 33). He knows that a mediator is required to approach God. The New Testament states that Jesus Christ is our Mediator, being both God and man, both divine and human: 'For there is one God and one Mediator between God and men, the Man Christ Jesus, who gave Himself a ransom for all' (1 Tim. 2:5–6). Jesus Christ's substitutionary atonement for sinners was necessary in order to sanctify a people unto God. The High Priestly work of Christ as Mediator allows sinners to reach heaven with the assurance of acceptance (Heb. 4:14–16; 10:19–25). Evidence of the forensic nature of justification recurs in the Scriptures, such as in Habakkuk 2:4: 'The just shall live by his faith.' Here we have the revelation of God's saving righteousness that is by faith alone. In Romans 1, Paul quotes these words from Habakkuk, believing that they are a call to trust in God's promises: 'For I am not ashamed of the gospel of Christ, for it is the power of God to salvation for everyone who believes, for the Jew first and also for the Greek. For in it the righteousness of God is revealed from faith to faith; as it is written, "The just shall live by faith"' (Rom. 1:16–17).

God is not reconciled to us by prayers or penances (acts of mortification of the flesh followed by absolution from a priest), but through faith in the atoning work of the one Mediator, Jesus Christ: 'For ... when we were enemies we were reconciled to God through the death of His Son ... through whom we have now received the reconciliation' (Rom. 5:10–11). When Paul deals with Job's question 'how can a man be righteous before God?' (Job 9:2), he explains the great theme of justification by faith alone and speaks of its nature, its necessity and its fruit. This truth was rediscovered at the Protestant Reformation and made much of by the magisterial Reformer Martin Luther.

Job longs for a mediator to plead on his behalf with God (9:33). This suggests that he thought of someone *other* than God himself. Here is a strong and resolute hope for a mediator between God and his people. Ultimately, Job's longing for this third party was fulfilled in Jesus Christ (1 Tim. 2:5). Under the influence of the Holy Spirit, Job is lifted out of his misery and given an eye to the future and to the coming Redeemer. Faith inspires hope, and hope does not disappoint (Rom. 5:5). He believes in a coming Saviour: 'And He shall stand at last on the earth' (19:25b). He holds on in faith and hope, and is comforted by the Spirit to look away from his situation to his Redeemer and the promise he brings with him.

Job remains angry (10:1–22)

In this chapter Job, feeling that he is without a mediator, carries on with his own defence. His mood has become more solemn and he expresses his loss of heart: 'My soul loathes my life; I will give free course to my complaint, I will speak in the bitterness of my soul. I will say to God, "Do not condemn me; show me why You contend with me"' (vv. 1–2).

Job is reminding us here that the people of God, until they learn better, like to think that they are in charge of their own destiny. However, the Christian must learn to trust God not just sometimes, or most times, but at all times (Ps. 62:8). This is an act of faith as well as a work of sanctifying grace.

Job now raises the issue about God ignoring the sins of the wicked but punishing the sins of his people: 'Does it seem good to You that You should oppress, that You should despise the work of Your hands, and smile on the counsel of the wicked?' (v. 3).

His protestations flow from his emotionally drained state and his endeavour to make sense of his prolonged sufferings to which God seems indifferent. Recovering from bereavement takes time—often a long time. Added to this, his long-lasting physical discomfort brought on by a chronic illness makes it seem as if God does not care about him. Job believes that God knows he is not guilty of wilful sin—because God knows all things. He is an omniscient Being (v. 7); so why is he (Job) so drained of energy, oppressed, disgraced, miserable and bitter (vv. 1, 15)? We see here a man whose emotional and mental state is so shot through and his annoyance so intense that they temporarily override his fear of God. Others have been angry with God; they include Jonah, who desired to die because God wanted him to do what he was very unwilling to do as an ordained prophet (Jonah 4:4). King David was angry with God because he thought that God had acted unjustly with Uzzah when he steadied the ark of God (2 Sam. 6:8). Job feels that God has acted unjustly towards him and so he asks the question again, 'Why me?' Anger can force us to blow up or shut up, and has the potential to create

alienation and bitterness (Gen. 4:6). However, there is such a
thing as righteous anger. The Bible reveals that not all anger
is sinful: 'Be angry, and do not sin' (Ps. 4:4; Eph. 4:26). God
is often angry, being, 'angry with the wicked every day' (Ps.
7:11)—but there is no unrighteousness with God. The people
of God are called to love righteousness and hate injustice
and evil. Although Job is bitter (10:1; 9:18), yet he is still
a believer, so he prays and takes everything to the Lord in
prayer. The people of God must do likewise, calling on God
and making use of the many promises related to prayer in
both Old and New Testaments. They must not be ignorant
of them or hesitant to use them. For example: 'It shall come
to pass that before they call, I will answer; and while they are
still speaking, I will hear' (Isa. 65:24); 'Let us therefore come
boldly to the throne of grace, that we may obtain mercy and
find grace to help in time of need' (Heb. 4:16).

Job's questions are candid, yet God does not condemn
him; rather he responds with grace and firmness. Job comes
to his Father in heaven. His struggles are those of a believer
and his humble faith will keep him on the straight and narrow
(2:10). When bereavement, pain and dark providences are
upon the people of God, they must believe that he will carry
them through.

FOR FURTHER STUDY

1. Read chapter 8 and describe Bildad's approach to adversity. How does Job answer him?

2. The concept of a mediator is found throughout the Scriptures. What is it, why is one needed, and what does our Mediator achieve? See Job 8:22; 9:33; 33:23; 1 Timothy 2:5; Hebrews 7:25; 12:24.

3. In what portions of the Bible can we find encouragement to pray when times are difficult and Heaven seems to be ignoring our prayers?

TO THINK ABOUT AND DISCUSS

1. Was the fact that Job was ill for months a factor in his friend's criticism? If so, what should be our reaction to those who have long-term illness?

2. Have you ever been angry with God? If so, how did it come about, and how did you deal with it?

3. Job was at ease approaching and speaking to God in prayer. Are you? On what grounds are we accepted and heard by him?

6 Job's dialogues

(11:1–17:16)

In this chapter we will consider some of the most famous and spiritually helpful words from Job's dialogues with his friends during his time of trial.

Zophar's first speech (11:1–20)

> Should not the multitude of words be answered?
> And should a man full of talk be vindicated?
> Should your empty talk make men hold their peace?
> And when you mock, should no one rebuke you?
> For you have said,
> 'My doctrine is pure,
> And I am clean in your eyes.'
>
> vv. 2–4

Zophar is the third friend to speak and he accuses Job of empty talk and of not taking his acquaintances seriously. He tells Job he is getting off lightly (vv. 1–6). Zophar acknowledges that God's greatness, transcendence and omniscience are true divine attributes (vv. 7–9). Sadly, he is as unsupportive as the other two friends and calls on Job to repent (vv. 10–20). He is right to urge repentance, but he fails to sympathize with Job's plight and pain. He cannot see that God always deals with his children in love, even through chastening. Zophar is 'dogmatic, cold, heartless and unfair in his accusations'.[1] He is like Mr Talkative in John Bunyan's *Pilgrim's Progress*: full of hot air and devoid of the knowledge of his own personal sinfulness. These tendencies force him to speak bluntly and nullify his attempts to help his friend. We must beware against a harshness of spirit.

Job's spiritual battle (12:1–14:22)

By chapter 12, the three friends have all spoken in a first round of attempts to help Job out of his misery. Eliphaz has relied on a dream for the basis of his wisdom (4:12–21); Bildad has trusted the tradition of the ancients (8:8–10); and Zophar has argued on dogmatic assumptions from his view of the transcendence of God (11:4–6). Together they present a combined view that Job is suffering because of his own personal sins. Job cannot bear this onslaught and in a caustic way accuses his friends of intellectual conceit: 'No doubt you are the people, and wisdom will die with you!' (12:2).

His friends may mean well, but they patronize and humiliate him. Job is now utterly fed up with this treatment and resorts to cynicism. He is not convinced that Zophar has any greater understanding than he has; he believes that he is his equal: 'But I have understanding as well as you; I am not inferior to you' (12:3; compare 13:2). It is evident that Job disagrees with his so-called friends' theology and their conclusions regarding the reasons for his bereavement, losses and illness. Instead of working with Job to help him, they are acting like opponents in a boxing ring who take him on, one at a time! However, Job may seem to be losing the argument, but God has provided these men in order to help him find his way through this trial, even though they are not up to the challenge (42:7). We know that Job, as one who is righteous in God's eyes (1:8), has more light than they have and holds the moral high ground. In response to Zophar, Job preaches a sermon whose topic is the nature and power of God (12:13–25). This is recognition that God is the Sovereign Lord, the one who does on earth and among the armies of heaven what he wills and whom no one can stop (Dan. 4:35).

A wrong diagnosis (13:1–28)

Job sees his friends as unfaithful to the true doctrine of God plainly displayed in creation (Ps. 19; Isa. 6:3b). He also states that they are proving most unhelpful to him personally: 'What you know, I also know; I am not inferior to you. But I would speak to the Almighty, and I desire to reason with God. But you forgers of lies, you are all worthless physicians' (vv. 2–4).

The friends have made a wrong diagnosis concerning the cause of Job's disease and sufferings, so he rejects their counsel and conclusions. Instead of piously accusing their unfortunate friend of personal transgression, the three should have been praying for God to supply grace in time of need. In fact, we know that their accusations served only to make themselves look good as their theological perspective implied that since Job was suffering and they were not, they were better than him. Wrong diagnosis leads to wrong treatment, and Job's friends have been administering the wrong medicine. Job's opinion is clear and his response forthright: 'Oh, that you would be silent, and it would be your wisdom!' (v. 5).

He also asks them to pay attention to his thoughts: 'Now hear my reasoning, and heed the pleadings of my lips' (vv. 6, 13, 17). If we wish to help others, it is necessary to listen to them and to pray with them. Job rebukes their pride and accuses them of partiality: 'Will you speak wickedly for God, and talk deceitfully for Him? Will you show partiality for Him? Will you contend for God?' (vv. 7–8). If we are to speak for God, there must be a knowledge of our own sins, to instil humility; a heart renewed by grace, to implant the kindness of love; and the unction of the Spirit, to deliver the truth.

Job endeavours to trust God at all times, saying, 'Though He slay me, yet will I trust Him' (v. 15). This verse is a powerful statement of Job's trust in God. Job is sure of his access to God (v. 16) and has a relationship that makes the heart glad. The people of God are called daily to conquer their fears through trust in the Bible's promises. This is both a challenge and the victory provided in Jesus that believers know. Satan attacks, but putting on the helmet of salvation every day will secure victory for Christ's redeemed people (Eph. 6:17). No matter how hot the battle, the Christian knows that ultimate victory is sure. Assurance of eventual deliverance brings peace, hope and patience (Rom. 8:31). We must trust Jesus Christ to forgive us when we repent (1 John 1:9), to forget our trespasses when we believe and to fill us with his Spirit for ministry (Luke 11:13; Acts 2:38; 5:32).

Job has decided (for the moment) that all his troubles flow from the fact that God is against him. Is it possible, he wonders, that personal sin and transgressions are the cause of his troubles? 'How many are my iniquities and sins? Make me know my transgression and my sin' (v. 23).

The three words used by Job—'sins', 'iniquities' and 'transgressions'—tell us that Job has a true biblical understanding of what sin is. *Sin* is to miss the mark, knowingly or unknowingly; *iniquity* is the want of integrity and righteousness; and *transgression* is wilful rebellion against God 'by crossing over the boundary of right and entering into the land of wrong'.[2]

The brevity of life (14:1–22)

Job continues his reply to Zophar by acknowledging that men and women have an eternal problem—namely their sin and its consequences: 'Man who is born of woman is of few days and full of trouble. He comes forth like a flower and fades away; he flees like a shadow and does not continue' (vv. 1–2).

> A sober assessment of the inevitability of death, linked with the fear of God, is the beginning of wisdom.

The doctrine of original sin is biblical and it must be understood not as a hindrance to salvation, but rather as an incentive to seeking forgiveness and cleansing through the blood of Jesus Christ. The gospel offers peace with God through Jesus Christ. A sober assessment of the inevitability of death, linked with the fear of God, is the beginning of wisdom. Job struggles with his relationship with God, not because he does not know God but because he has a genuine fear of God and he wants answers to his questions before death. Job's point here is that time is not our own to do with what we like: 'Since his [man's] days are determined, the number of his months is with You; You have appointed his limits, so that he cannot pass' (v. 5).

Job agrees with Eliphaz's assessment back in 5:7 that 'man is born to trouble, as the sparks fly upward', so he stresses life's misery and brevity through two vivid similes: 'like a [fading] flower' and 'like a [fleeing] shadow' (v. 2). The truth that God determines the length of a person's life (v. 5) emphasizes God's sovereign power and wisdom, and conversely the impotence of human beings under divinely set limits. We must be aware that Job is not thinking of fatalism: that is not a scriptural idea. God has decreed that believing prayer and the work of the Holy Spirit urging faith in the promises of the Scriptures are always factors in his providential care (Luke 7:9, 50). Job's thoughts here also emphasize the need to remember that 'all in Adam die'—that is, by imputation, the first sin of Adam renders all his descendants guilty before God, resulting in their death (Ps. 51:5; Rom 5:12–14).

Job complains to God (15:1–17:16)

Eliphaz's second speech, in chapter 15, offers no comfort to Job: 'Your own mouth condemns you, and not I; Yes, your own lips testify against you' (v. 6).

He piles on the pressure, trying to make Job acknowledge that he has been wicked and foolish. Here again we see that Eliphaz is wrong. He speaks out of ignorance and with a boldness that is not warranted. He is not the man to help Job: this we now clearly see. How can Eliphaz say such things about Job, especially when he is regarded by him as a friend? Surely it is because he is not actually listening to Job or considering the facts, but instead is full of his own pompous opinions! As a result, Job now feels the rod of the Almighty more acutely. We have his response to Eliphaz in chapters 16–17.

The real adversary (16:1–22)

Job firstly addresses the friends with these words: 'I have heard many such things; miserable comforters are you all!' (v. 2).

Not coping well with their criticism, Job then complains to God, 'My friends scorn me; my eyes pour out tears to God' (v. 20; see also v. 16). Charles H. Spurgeon has come this way too:

> Who are these people who scorn you? They *are your friends*, and that makes it the harder to bear. Caesar said, 'Et tu, Brute!'—'And thou, Brutus! Dost thou stab?' So, too, one of our Lord's sharpest griefs was, '*He that eateth bread with me* hath lifted up his heel against me.' It is hard for a young Christian to be persecuted by the father to whose judgment he has always looked up with respect. Harder still is it for a Christian woman to find the partner of her bosom steeled against her for the truth's sake. Oh! how they can get at our hearts, these husbands and these wives of ours, and if they happen to be enemies of Christ, what wounds they can make! 'My friends scorn me.' You would not mind if it were merely

the workpeople in the shop. You could escape from them, but you cannot escape from your own family.[3]

In verse 9 Job speaks of 'my adversary': 'He tears me in His wrath, and hates me; He gnashes at me with His teeth; My adversary sharpens His gaze on me.' Satan is the true adversary of God's people. Job feels that he is wrestling with God, but God is not in the ring! He has yet to trust God fully and at all times (Ps. 62:8), to let him have his way in his life and to sing praises to him in his long, lonely nights of darkness. For the remainder of chapter 16 to the end of chapter 17 he addresses God and complains about his conflict of faith.

The words of Job in verses 9–22 take the believer to the cross. Spoken prophetically by Job, they reveal that he is sharing in the fellowship of Christ's sufferings. This is God's plan for all God's children, as revealed by the apostles Paul and Peter in their epistles (2 Cor. 1:7; 1 Peter 4:12–13). Job is sure that the truth about himself—his faith, attitudes and hope—are known in heaven: 'Surely even now my witness is in heaven, and my evidence is on high' (v. 19).

The real Judge (17:1–16)

Job is teetering on the edge of death as his friends mock him (vv. 1–2). He wants God alone to try his case because his critics have proven themselves to be of no comfort. He cannot find one wise man among his three antagonists (v. 10). The Lord, he feels, has made him an object of contempt (v. 6), so he wants God to vindicate him before he dies. Using a legal metaphor, Job appeals to God to act as his barrister by laying down a pledge, resulting in release from his pain while he waits for the

Judge's verdict: 'Now put down a pledge for me with Yourself. Who is he who will shake hands with me?' (v. 3).

Perhaps Job and the apostle Paul shared the same experience among proud and self-opinionated men whose knowledge of God was elementary and whose understanding of the ways of God was less than perfect. Paul's relationship with many inside the church at Corinth was at best cool and at worst hostile (on their side), and Job and his friends were in a similar relationship; thus Job could no doubt have echoed Paul's words:

> But with me it is a very small thing that I should be judged by you or by a human court. In fact, I do not even judge myself. For I know of nothing against myself, yet I am not justified by this; but He who judges me is the Lord. Therefore judge nothing before the time, until the Lord comes, who will both bring to light the hidden things of darkness and reveal the counsels of the hearts. Then each one's praise will come from God.
>
> 1 Cor. 4:3–5

As a steward under God and responsible to him, Job was not worried about the useless comments of those around him (although he found them offensive and painful); this was because the ultimate Judge is the Lord himself. Since God is Judge, we should be careful not to make any untimely evaluations of others. That is why it was a very small thing that Paul should be judged by mortal and fallible humans. The safest policy is to judge 'nothing before the time', but to wait 'until the Lord comes' (1 Cor. 4:5). He will judge not only what is seen by the eye, but also the motives of the hearts: not only *what* was done, but *why* it was done. Job, if deserving of praise, will receive praise from God and not from men. 'We know that Job's sorrows were recorded, not for his honour, but for our profit. We are told to consider the patience of Job, and truly we might often be sustained, cheered, and comforted if we would but look upon that patriarch in the depths of his grief.'[4]

Chapters 16–17 close the first round of dialogue between Job and his friends. It has brought Job even lower and had an impact on his self-esteem, so he complains, 'He has made me a byword of the people' (17:6).

For further study ▶

1. Find Scripture passages that use the different words for 'sin' in the Old Testament. How would you define these words' meanings according to the contexts in which they are used?

2. What do the trials of faith tell us about God's people sharing in the sufferings of Christ (see 2 Cor. 1:7; 1 Peter 4:12–13)? What are the implications of this?

3. Paul teaches that we do not wrestle against flesh and blood (Eph. 6:12). How does this fit with Job's trials (Job 13)?

TO THINK ABOUT AND DISCUSS

1. How should we respond when people will not accept the truth and argue against us wrongly?

2. Why did Eliphaz, apparently Job's friend, say such nasty things about Job? Was it because he was not listening to the facts and was full of his own opinions? Have you ever experienced anything like this? How can you make sure you don't behave in the same way towards others?

3. Consider the statements 'Judge not, that you be not judged' (Matt. 7:1) and '… judge nothing before the time' (1 Cor. 4:5). What are the implications for our relationships?

7 Job's hope

(18:1–19:29)

In chapter 18 we find Bildad in dialogue with
Job for a second time. He feels that Job
debates too much and does not know what he
is talking about: 'How long till you put an end
to words?' (v. 2).

There are irreconcilable differences between
Job and his friends. Bildad here shows that he
has the same attitude to Job as Eliphaz had in
15:2: 'Should a wise man answer with empty
knowledge, and fill himself with the east wind?' With blunt
and unjust language Bildad also likens Job to the wicked
(18:5–21), who, he says, are to blame for their own failures
(v. 7), are afflicted by disease (v. 13), are quickly forgotten
(v. 17), have a shortened lifespan (v. 18) and lose all their
children before they themselves die: 'He has neither son
nor posterity among his people, nor any remaining in
his dwellings' (v. 19). He concludes, 'Surely such are the
dwellings of the wicked, and this is the place of him who

does not know God' (v. 21). Job is in his sights and he pulls the trigger!

Job's sufferings (19:1–24)

Job remains perplexed about his troubles, is losing hope, and is now expecting to die, as he stated in chapter 17: 'My spirit is broken, my days are extinguished, the grave is ready for me' (17:1).

His friends, to their own satisfaction, have apparently proved their case that Job is guilty before God—that is, he has deliberately sinned against the laws of the Almighty (13:23). Job, however, cannot find in himself a rational explanation for his sorrows except that God has for some unknown reason caught him in a net and there is no way of escape (19:4–6). He now concludes that his friends are against him, his wife is against him, God appears to be against him, and even those to whom he has shown kindness are ignoring him (vv. 11–20). As a consequence, he is losing hope and coming to the edge of unbelief. His trials have brought him very low, filling him with despair; he has reached the lowest point in this episode of his life. In this condition of despondency he imagines that there is no way of escape (v. 12). In such hopeless despair, the people of God are tempted to doubt Christ's love and promises. It is all too much, and Job cries for pity and sympathy from his companions and the others whom he has mentioned (v. 21). Job now feels very alone and abandoned; even his wife is a stranger.

Trials can make one feel very lonely. Loneliness is hard to bear, and husbands and wives are meant to be loving and faithful to each other at all times; this is why God said, 'It is not good that man should be alone' (Gen. 2:18). Being forsaken by those we love and respect is the worst of experiences. We can expect such treatment from our enemies, but not from our nearest and dearest. Yet this is what Job is going through.

Yet, despite his feelings telling him that God is not listening to his complaints, Job holds on to eternal life, and hope springs eternal because of faith in his Redeemer (vv. 25–27). Hope is an essential ingredient in the faith of the people of God (1 Cor. 13:13), while hopelessness is a dreadful affliction.

Sharing in Christ's sufferings

Reading chapter 19 cannot but remind the Christian of the sufferings and sorrow which our Saviour went through. Without realizing it, Job was sharing in Christ's sufferings. He did not know that this was ordained for him as a believer; all he knew was that he had faith in God, so why was he suffering like he was? Was God angry with him? We know that people can become very low and depressed in times of sorrow, yet God permits

> Without realizing it, Job was sharing in Christ's sufferings.

this to happen to them. Charles H. Spurgeon, commenting on Exodus 3:7 ('And the LORD said: "I have surely seen the oppression of My people who are in Egypt, and have heard their cry because of their taskmasters, for I know their sorrows"'), remarked,

> If you are in the dark, if your spirits are sunk in gloom, do not despair, for the Lord Jesus was there. If you have fallen

into misery, do not give up because the Father's well-beloved passed through deeper darkness … if you are under a cloud … trust Him, and He will cause his light to shine on you.[1]

All that the people of God go through and endure while here on earth comes to them in fellowship with their Saviour. They cannot escape this. It is not possible to live the Christian life and not share in the fellowship of Christ's sufferings. This is God's plan for his people, and their mystical union with Christ makes it inevitable (2 Cor. 1:7; 1 Peter 4:12–13). The fellowship of Christ's sufferings means sharing in the reproach, rejection, hostility and hatred that follow on from identification with Jesus Christ and bearing witness to him.

Job feels that his view of things should be written down so that posterity will be able to learn the truth. His 'comforters' will not listen, but others might. Others might come to the realization that he is innocent of all their unjust charges: 'Oh, that my words were written! Oh, that they were inscribed in a book! That they were engraved on a rock with an iron pen and lead, forever!' (vv. 23–24).

Those who have been in a similar position to that of Job will know how Job feels at this point. Was not Jesus Christ, our Saviour, also falsely accused, reviled and spat upon? Job shared in Christ's sufferings, being accused of sins he had not committed, and was reckoned guilty by his accusing companions. Job does not understand the charges against him, nor does he understand the evidence they claim to have. Because of this he seeks true justice (vv. 7, 11). Job's words have been saved for us in the text of Holy Scripture as a testimony to his righteousness, God's faithfulness and the Holy Spirit's regeneration. His friends did not respect his words, so he wanted them in print (v. 23).

Job's hope (19:25–29)

Job 19 is a key chapter as it evidences a turning point in Job's road to full recovery. His friends have proved to be unfaithful and tediously critical of him. Yet, instead of responding to Bildad's second speech with a sense of hopelessness, we find that Job's spirit rises to its highest point of anticipation and hope.

The resurrection

Job's belief in the resurrection of the body shines through despite all his troubles, pains and difficulties: 'For I know that my Redeemer lives, and He shall stand at last on the earth; and after my skin is destroyed, this I know, that in my flesh I shall see God, whom I shall see for myself, and my eyes shall behold, and not another. How my heart yearns within me!' (vv. 25–27).

Job's language is that of the believer. He is convinced that God is his Redeemer and that he will one day see God, whether in the flesh or out of it. When he does, God will be on his side as his Advocate. On these verses Matthew Henry says, 'Job was taught of God to believe in a living Redeemer, and to look for the resurrection of the dead and the life of the world to come.'[2] Job had lost all hope of getting physically better and he did not think that he would live much longer (vv. 8–10; see also 30:23). However, Job is under the influence of the Holy Spirit and as a result is lifted out of his misery and given an eye to the future. At this point Job rests in hope while exercising faith and patience. This hope is founded on the very character of the living God himself, and Job looks to him who is to come as his Advocate (Rom. 15:13; see also 1 John 2:1).

Job has a firm time line regarding the events of the Messianic second coming, as we shall see below. This proves that the hope of the people of God in the restoration of all creation after the fall into sin in the Garden of Eden is very ancient, dating back at least to the time of the patriarchs. It also shows the light that was blessed to Job because of the grace of God in his life. He is convinced that God is *his* Redeemer: 'For I know that *my* Redeemer lives' (v. 25, emphasis added). Note also that King David could say, 'The LORD [Jehovah] is *my* shepherd' (Ps. 23:1, emphasis added). These texts show that there was grace and light in the hearts of Old Testament saints.

> The hope of the people of God in the restoration of all creation after the fall into sin in the Garden of Eden is very ancient, dating back at least to the time of the patriarchs.

Where did such faith come from? Let us remember that the Old Testament speaks in many places about the resurrection from the dead (Job 14:14; 19:25–27; Ps. 16:9–11; 17:15; 49:8–9, 15; 73:24–26). Psalm 16 is quoted by Peter at Pentecost: 'For You will not leave my soul in Hades, nor will You allow Your Holy One to see corruption' (Acts 2:27). Other Old Testament references to the resurrection can be found in Isaiah 26:19; 53:10–12; Ezekiel 37:1–14;

Daniel 12:2, 13; Hosea 6:2; 13:14. The absence of proof
texts for the resurrection in the Pentateuch may at first seem
problematic until we remember that Jesus quoted Exodus
3:6 in Matthew's Gospel to prove that there is life after death
for the people of God:

> You are mistaken, not knowing the Scriptures nor the power
> of God. For in the resurrection they neither marry nor are
> given in marriage, but are like angels of God in heaven. But
> concerning the resurrection of the dead, have you not read
> what was spoken to you by God, saying, 'I am the God of
> Abraham, the God of Isaac, and the God of Jacob'? God is
> not the God of the dead, but of the living.
>
> Matt. 22:29–33

Christ was here responding to the Sadducees, who rejected
the doctrine of the resurrection. They were scholars who
majored on the five books of Moses and they had missed
this vital proof of the doctrine of the resurrection. Francis I.
Andersen comments,

> ... the argument that Job does not expect personal
> reconstitution as a man, because this idea entered Judaism
> only towards the very end of the biblical period, can be
> dismissed in the light of much recent research that shows
> interest in the after-life as an ancient concern for Israelite
> faith. In particular, the outcome of our study of such passages
> as Job 14:13ff., if valid, shows that the hope of resurrection
> lies at the very heart of Job's faith.[3]

The Sadducees also forgot about the resurrection in the
rest of the Old Testament; for example, when the widow of
Zarephath's son was brought back to life from the dead by
Elijah (1 Kings 17:20–22) and, similarly, the Shunammite

woman's son was raised by Elisha (2 Kings 4:32–35). In the New Testament we have the record of Jesus raising Jairus's daughter (Luke 8:40–56); Lazarus's resurrection (John 11:43–44); Peter raising Dorcas (Acts 9:40–41); and Paul with Eutychus (Acts 20:9-12). Both the Old and New Testaments, then, clearly understand and teach the resurrection of the body. These miracles are a type of the certainty to come at the second coming of the Lord Jesus Christ from heaven.

The second coming

The hope of the return of the Messiah lies at the very heart of Job's faith. He believes in a coming Saviour: 'And He shall stand at last on the earth' (v. 25b).

This is a reference to the last day. Whatever our lot in life, as Christians we can, like Job, believe in and yearn for heaven: '… whom I shall see for myself, and my eyes shall behold, and not another. How my heart yearns within me!' (v. 27).

As we have noted before, 'heart' in Hebrew signifies the seat of one's emotions; thus Job yearns for death's release and heaven's joys. But even more, he is assured by faith, as a child of God, that he will see his Redeemer. During extreme suffering, this hope is God-given and Holy Spirit-inspired so that God's people find comfort in the gospel itself. As Paul says, God is the 'God of hope' (Rom. 15:13; see also Titus 2:13; 3:7). Job's hope anticipates the fulfilment of the promises of God (John 11:25). Notice the prophetic time line:

- The return of the Redeemer: 'For I know that my Redeemer lives, and He shall stand at last on the earth.'

- The resurrection of the redeemed: 'And after my skin is destroyed, this I know, that in my flesh I shall see God.'
- The fullness of redemption: '… whom I shall see for myself, and my eyes shall behold, and not another.'

This is the time line planned for the return of the Saviour (Redeemer) Jesus Christ; it is also set out by Paul in 1 Thessalonians 4:13–17. Job does not regard his Redeemer as a local cultic deity but as the eternal, living Creator of all things. He holds on in faith and hope and is comforted by the Holy Spirit to look away from his situation to his Redeemer and the promise he brings with him.

Death is not the end for believers; at death they are taken immediately into heaven (Phil. 1:21–23; 2 Cor. 5:8). In heaven (the intermediate state), the redeemed saints of God await the resurrection at the last day (John 5:28–30; 1 Cor. 15:42–49; 1 John 3:2). Job is a pilgrim. This world is not his home: he looks forward to heaven, trusting in the living God, his Kinsman-Redeemer (see Ruth 4:5–8).[4]

For further study ▶

1. Write out those Old Testament verses which speak of bodily resurrection.

2. Read Philippians 3:10; 2 Corinthians 1:7; 1 Peter 4:12–13. What is meant by 'the sufferings of Christ', and why, according to these verses, do Christians share in them?

3. Psalm 78:35 speaks of God as Israel's Redeemer (see also Ps. 119:154; and Ruth 4:1, where the same Hebrew word is translated as 'close relative'). The 'Kinsman-Redeemer' is the one appointed by God to redeem his kin from difficulty and danger (Ps. 19:14; 78:35; Prov. 23:11; Jer. 50:34). How does Jesus Christ fit this role?

TO THINK ABOUT AND DISCUSS

1. The Christian hope of resurrection is preached less than his death on the cross. Why is this so? Do you think that the balance should be changed? Discuss.

2. Job believed in the resurrection of the body long before Christ's resurrection. How could he do so? When you are going through hard times, does the hope of the resurrection help you?

3. How often do you think about Christ's second coming? If you thought about it more, would it make any difference to the way you live your life?

8 Job's theology

(20:1–24:25)

Zophar's second speech (ch. 20) is his response to Job's discourse in chapter 19 and contains words of harsh contempt rather than humility with respect. One commentator regards it as 'cold, cruel and heartless'.[1]

Zophar sees God as a God of vengeance who exercises wrath against the wicked. This is evident in the lack of love, mercy or compassion in his words. Thus the sufferings of Job are great because he is a great sinner! Great sufferers are great sinners! This attitude is flawed, but sadly many are guilty of thinking the same way, even today. Job rejects this unenlightened theology.

Job's strengthened faith (21:1–22:30)

His rejection of his friends' understanding (21:1–34)

Job's seventh speech in chapter 21 begins to deal directly with the view of the three friends that all suffering is punishment from God because of personal sinfulness. The friends have misrepresented God and have not dealt with the theology of personal suffering in a correct manner. Nor have they understand why Job is suffering now. Here we see the great contrast in theological understanding between Job and these friends. Job takes Zophar's tirade about the fate of the wicked (ch. 20) as his lead and develops a more scriptural view of God's dealings with the wicked, which once again exposes the three as unenlightened men, despite their claim to be the opposite. It is true that the wicked do not always have a good death, but they often appear to do so (v. 13). Job concludes by saying that his friends speak with duplicity: 'How then can you comfort me with empty words, since falsehood remains in your answers?' (v. 34).

These words expose Job's considered conclusion about the three, and it is not a favourable one. Job now understands that they are unable to help him while they hold on to a theology that excludes the notion of a personal God who is full of grace. Their thesis is proved wrong by their rejection of Job's own testimony and by their lack of a personal knowledge of the living God in the soul. Those who object to this analysis must remember that all who have ever known God by faith did so by way of supernatural grace, whether in the time of the Old Testament or the New (Ps. 23:1–6; Hab. 2:4; Heb. 10:37–39).

Eliphaz's misrepresentation of Job (22:1–30)

In Eliphaz's third speech he is still attempting to convince Job that he, Eliphaz, is wise and has understanding of the things of God; so he challenges Job to answer some questions, while again repeating his assertion that Job is not as righteous as he thinks he is: 'Is not your wickedness great, and your iniquity without end?' (v. 5).

Job is accused of greedy exploitation of the poor and a lack of charity and compassion towards the bereaved (vv. 6–11). Eliphaz misrepresents Job's position and twists his words to say that God is so distant from us, being outside the earth's atmosphere, that he cannot see our wickedness (vv. 13–14).[2] Eliphaz issues another call for repentance, urging Job to trust in God and not in money or his acquired riches (vv. 23–24). Eliphaz's accusations are fabrications of his spiritual poverty. Job, however, is not guilty. He is very frustrated by the way Eliphaz and the others twist his statements. No matter how much he speaks to them and does his best to be open and clear, the three fail to understand what he is meaning. This is a spiritual problem on their part. Their worldview is different because they do not know God experimentally. Job's only solution is to continue to trust God at all times, to be patient in his sorrows, and to stay calm.

Job's personal feelings (23:1–17)

Job's yearning (vv. 1–9)

Job still remains perplexed by his trials and the providences of God that have brought them about. Neither does he understand why the wicked get away with their sins in this life and the righteous suffer while alive. When he prays, he feels that heaven does not hear and God is silent, and he longs that it might be otherwise: 'Even today my complaint is bitter; my hand is listless because of my groaning. Oh, that I knew where I might find Him, that I might come to His seat!' (vv. 2–3).

Job longs for the opportunity to state his case before God. He does not claim absolute innocence; rather he seeks light and truth and expects to be vindicated as far as his three friends are concerned. God is his Redeemer (19:25–27), so he expects to be listened to and accepted as a justified sinner, righteous in God sight (vv. 4–7; compare 1:8; 2:3). Job cannot understand why God is delaying his response and help: 'Look, I go forward, but He is not there, and backward, but I cannot perceive Him; when He works on the left hand, I cannot behold Him; when He turns to the right hand, I cannot see Him' (vv. 8–9).

As we have said, all Job can do, as the prisoner of the Lord, is continue to trust God, be patient in his sorrows and stay composed. Or, as the common saying puts it, 'Keep calm and carry on'.

Job's assurance (vv. 10–17)

> But He knows the way that I take;
> When He has tested me, I shall come forth as gold.

v. 10

Job now 'affirms his integrity and his faithfulness to God's Word'.[3] Having searched his own heart, Job can find no unfaithfulness, nor any rejection of God's Word. On the contrary, he orders his life after God's own precepts. He is in step with the apostle Paul, who believed that God would complete the work of grace in his people (Phil. 1:6). This is about God's plan for Job's life. Charles H. Spurgeon remarked, 'If one severe trial does not sanctify you, expect another more rigorous.'[4] The intense heat of the refiner's fire guarantees only pure gold: 'I shall come forth as gold.' God's covenant of redemption promises a spotless bride for the Redeemer (Phil. 1:6; Rev. 21:2, 9).

Job's progress in understanding God's dealings with his children provokes a new question: 'What now?' This in turn introduces new hope and shifts Job's focus from himself to God and what God is doing in his life. God wants only the best for his people, and they must believe this is so and trust in Christ Jesus for the future. Our times are in his hands (Ps. 31:15). Because of his personal relationship with God, Job finds an understanding of the truth of sanctification through his trials. He now begins to comprehend the answers to the questions 'Why me?' and 'Why now?' He also begins to grasp that sanctification is an ongoing process and requires those who love God to let Christ have his way in their lives. This is because the people of God are called to walk by faith and to cooperate with the Holy Spirit. They are to live in the Spirit, walk in the Spirit and be led by him (Gal. 5:25, 18). Job's fears are not realized: he understands that God is on his side.

> My times are in Thy hand;
> My God, I wish them there;
> My life, my friends, my soul I leave
> Entirely to Thy care.

My times are in Thy hand;
Whatever they may be;
Pleasing or painful, dark or bright,
As best may seem to Thee.

My times are in Thy hand;
Why should I doubt or fear?
My Father's hand will never cause
His child a needless tear.

My times are in Thy hand,
I'll always trust in Thee;
And, after death, at Thy right hand
I shall forever be.[5]

Job's view of the wicked (24:1–45)

The topic of the character and prosperity of the wicked has
been a recurring theme up to this point. In chapters 20, 21
and 22, Zophar, Job and Eliphaz, respectively, have spoken
about it, and now in chapter 24 Job comes back again to this
perennial theological hot chestnut, namely, 'Why do the
wicked prosper, and why do the righteous suffer, and why
does God not do something about both?'

Job asks questions about the prosperity of the wicked in
this world. They appear not to be punished for their wicked
deeds, instead seeming to prosper while rejecting the truth,
rebelling against the light and living without the fear of God
in their hearts. He thinks especially about murderers and
adulterers who fear only the human consequences of their

actions: they should not get away with their sins on earth. Although God delays their punishment, he believes that God will deal with them in his own time, even if they are prosperous for a little while (vv. 24–25).

Job wants the wicked to be held responsible for their actions. Yet it appears that God overlooks wicked people's treatment of the helpless and is indifferent to their sufferings. Job begins by saying that it looks as if God pays no attention to the wickedness of the ungodly who remove the 'landmarks' (v. 2), exploit the poor (vv. 3–8) and kidnap children (vv. 9–11): 'Yet God does not charge them with wrong' (v. 12). Murderers (v. 14), adulterers (v. 15) and thieves (v. 16) all get away with their crimes in their lifetimes. Why does God not hold them responsible and judge them? Where are the police officers and judges to deal with this? Meanwhile, the wicked keep sinning and the righteous still suffer injustice; greed and exploitation of the poor and the weak go on and on and on. In this complaint Job questions the morality of suffering in a world created by a just and loving God.

Unanswered, this question causes many to reject the faith of God's elect and to remain in despair. For others, it is a convenient excuse for not believing in and yielding to God. Job's answer is that the wicked will *not* get away with it! Yes, they will get their comeuppance. God will judge all people, even the wicked and the powerful (vv. 18–24). To sum up:

- Job believes that the wicked reject a caring God and he observes, on the part of the wicked, an arrogant hostility towards God: 'Yet they say to God, "Depart from us, for we do not desire the knowledge of Your ways. Who is the Almighty, that we should serve Him? And what profit do we have if we pray to Him?' (21:14–15). The wicked work at night (24:15) and they kill, steal and rape. They are children of darkness: 'they do not know the light' (v. 16b). Satan, greed and selfish desires drive them on to sinfulness. The wicked are defined not only as evil-doers, but also as being blind to spiritual realities. If the blind lead the blind, they will both fall into a ditch (Matt. 15:14)! They are always learning but never coming to the knowledge of the truth (2 Tim. 3:7).

- Job knows that the wicked reject eternal life, but he cannot understand why the judgement day is delayed. This is still a problem for many Christians today, as well as for those who are unsaved. Will justice be triumphant? Job is confident that it will—but not yet! He knows that 'There are those who rebel against the light; they do not know its ways nor abide in its paths' (v. 13). The Bible says that God 'commands all men everywhere to repent' (Acts 17:30). Repentance is a turning from past sins and is accompanied by an inner resolve to trust in Jesus Christ for forgiveness and peace through the power of the Holy Spirit.

- Job understands that the wicked reject holy living and divine truth, and he expects a day of reckoning. 'They are exalted for a little while, then they are gone. They are brought low; they are taken out of the way like all others; they dry out like the heads of grain' (v. 24). God is righteous and his judgements are always good, holy and just: 'For the wicked are reserved for the day of doom; they shall be brought out on the day of wrath' (21:30).

The psalmist noted, 'God is angry with the wicked every day' (Ps 7:11). A wilful and conscious rejection of God is a cold shoulder towards fellowship with him. The wicked do not pray for salvation and see no benefit at all in such a concept. God gives time to repent (2 Peter 3:9), but will they humble themselves and ask for forgiveness as transgressors of his laws?

For further study ▶

1. Read chapters 20–24. How would you sum up the Book of Job's view of the wicked?
2. In Job 22:14, is Eliphaz saying that the earth is round? If so, how did he know (see also Isa. 40:22)? Look at the use of the Hebrew word for 'circle' ('sphere'; see Job 22:14; Prov. 8:27; Isa. 40:22) to form a conclusion.

TO THINK ABOUT AND DISCUSS

1. If you were to argue against the notion that all suffering is punishment from God, which Scripture passages could you use?
2. 'Why do the wicked live and become old, yes, become mighty in power?' (21:7). Does this still happen today? Give examples. What answer would you give to this question?
3. In what way does asking the question, 'What now?' help us to move on after tragedy or severe illness?
4. Job 23:10 is a precious verse, speaking of the believer's assurance. How can you make sure you remember this verse in a time of testing? Is there someone you can encourage today with its truth?

9 Job's wisdom

(25:1–31:40)

Bildad's insults continue with his (very short) third speech in chapter 25. He insinuates that Job is wrong in declaring his innocence (v. 4).

He asks, 'How then can man be righteous before God?' Is his comment that a 'son of man' is 'a worm' (25:6) reinforced in his mind because Job is covered in worms (7:5)? What is clear is that this question exposes Bildad's lack of spiritual light. He believes in God and in judgement to come; however, the righteousness of God revealed from faith to faith eludes him because he has not yet grasped that salvation is by faith alone (Hab. 2:4). His speech has no relevance to Job's plight and adds nothing new (26:2). Neither he nor his friends can contend with Job's optimism or his constant claim to be righteous. Nor can they understand this. For this reason I would describe them as nominal believers—believers in name only. Yes, they believe in an all-powerful God as a truism, and the Creator God as the judge of all the living and the dead; nevertheless, there is no knowledge of personal forgiveness and peace with God through the Mediator. Job's consistent witness and testimony to his own (imputed) righteousness has at last, it seems, raised a question in Bildad's mind about being right with God—a concept he cannot yet grasp but one he now wonders about.

His question is rhetorical; he knows very well that all men and women fall short of the glory of God. Job does not respond to Bildad's comments and insults; rather, in chapter 26 he continues where he left off in chapter 24.

Job's remarkable statements (26:1–14)

The Book of Job contains some remarkable statements about the world we live in. How is it that Job knew that God, as Creator, 'stretches out the north over empty space; He hangs the earth on nothing' (v. 7)?

What prompted this understanding? It is probable that Job and the others learned about God from observing the stellar heavens, just as the psalmist did (Ps. 19:1–6; see also Job 9:9); we call this knowledge 'natural revelation'. However, they would also have learned from oral tradition about the creation (26:7), the flood (22:16), what happened to Sodom and Gomorrah (22:20), and that the earth was a sphere (22:14; Isa. 40:22). In Job's day there was no canon of Scripture in existence, but it is certain that Job and his friends saw the glory of the Creator in God's handiwork (no light pollution in those days). These men knew more about God's creation than their progeny.[1]

They also observed that the earth's northern axis points to the pole star. The 'empty space' (v. 7; translated as 'the void' in the ESV) comes from the same word translated as 'without form' in Genesis 1:2, 'referring to the formless condition of the original matter of the earth when God first called into existence the space/time/mass universe (Gen. 1:1)', says Morris.[2] The words 'He hangs the earth on nothing' (v. 7) means that there are no strings, pillars or supports of any kind. Other ancients suggested that the world was supported on the back of a cosmic tortoise or elephant, while the ancient Greeks believed that it was held up by the strong man Atlas. God's Word is correct and we know today that it is the force of gravity that holds the earth in space.[3] We must not think of Job and his companions as ignoramuses. It is obvious that they had an understanding of cosmology which was only observed when the Apollo 8 spacecraft, while on its way to the moon and back in 1968, photographed the earth from space and found it hanging on nothing.[4]

Job's integrity and wisdom (27:1–28:28)

The interaction Job has had with his friends up until now has helped him to grow in the realization that they have no valid case against him, so he becomes bolder and more assured of his own innocence. Thus we find him in a more bullish mood, continuing to uphold his innocence and committing himself to serve and follow the paths of holiness all his days on earth, showing a personal resolve to walk with God: 'Till I die I will not put away my integrity from me. My righteousness I hold fast, and will not let it go; my heart shall not reproach me as long as I live' (27:5b–6).

What Job is seeking is confirmation from God—in contradiction to what his friends have been saying to him—that his own relationship with God through faith is unimpaired. It is not built on personal merit through good deeds and penances. Job's expanding faith will now embrace his sufferings as something between himself and God within a right relationship. Still defending himself (27:7–12) Job seeks to correct his three friends, maintaining his directness of speech to challenge their unjust accusations and unwise conclusions: 'Surely all of you have seen it; why then do you behave with complete nonsense?' (27:12).

In chapter 28, Job discourses on the topic of wisdom; he speaks freely and from the heart, addressing both God and his friends. Job has been accused of trusting in his riches and not God. Now he deals with this accusation which must have cut him to the quick, as he knew in his heart that he trusted only in the living God for righteousness and life.

True wisdom comes from God (28:1–6). For Job, wisdom cannot be divorced from God's self-revelation. The wisdom of Job's friends is worldly and based on intuition and experience without revelation, and thus it has severe limitations. The wisdom Job speaks about is not known by the birds or beasts (lions, 28:8) nor is its shrewdness gained from man's longevity, but rather from God's grace in the heart and the living Word of God in the soul. Job asks, 'Where can wisdom be found?' (28:12); it cannot be bought (28:15), but it is understanding (28:20b) and ultimately found in the heart that fears God and understands

> Wisdom is not a product of intellect, learning or age, but the work of the Holy Spirit, being a gift of God ultimately found in Jesus Christ.

the need for holiness (28:28). Wisdom is not a product of intellect, learning or age, but the work of the Holy Spirit, being a gift of God ultimately found in Jesus Christ (Col. 1:9, 28; 4:5; 1 Cor. 2:6–7). Throughout Job's trials his worldview has been under attack, but Job is the only one to see that God is just and the justifier of those who believe in him. This is because he has insight and understanding that the others do not possess. Job's biblical righteousness is seen in his personal wisdom (28:28).

Job's self-defence (29:1–31:40)

As a member of the rich and affluent of his society, Job was part of a class of highly honoured and respected wise men (29:21). In these chapters Job makes a summary defence of his own righteousness. He does so by recounting the good old days when he was well respected and accepted among his peers and the citizens of his city (29:1–25). He speaks of the time not so long past when he:

- Had close fellowship with God (29:1–6)
- Was respected and liked in the city (29:7–10)
- Ministered to others (29:11–13)
- Was listened to by young and old, rich and poor (29:21–25)

Job at one time commanded respect near and far, and was acknowledged as first among equals (29:14). What is more, he was expecting to live a long and prosperous life (29:18–20)—but he has now been chastened. He took this for granted and as the norm, forgetting that his times were in Gods hands (Ps. 31:15). We must walk in the conscious recognition that all we have is a gift of God and belongs to us only temporarily (Prov. 3:5–7; Eccles. 3).

In chapter 30 Job asks another question: 'Why take this ministry and prominence from me, Lord? I was so well liked. I was doing well and was full of good works. Why, then, am I now confronted by and surrounded with these ignoramuses?' As he sits outside the city on its rubbish tip (2:8; 42:6b), Job is the receiver of mocking and contempt, and it is all so difficult to cope with: 'I am their taunting song' (30:9). Their comments have been so cutting, hurtful and snide. When one is the butt of the jokes of others and given the cold shoulder, it can be nearly impossible to bear. As a result he is deeply downcast (30:16) and feels once again that he has been cast off by God. God does not befriend him any more— where is God in all his suffering, pain and confusion? 'I cry out to You, but You do not answer me … You have become cruel to me; with the strength of Your hand You oppose me' (30:20–21).

Job is again letting off steam to get things off his chest:

- I don't deserve this (30:25).
- My heart is in turmoil (30:27).
- I cry for help (30:28).
- I am an outcast (30:29).
- I am full of disease (30:30).
- I have lost my joy (30:31).

Job feels abandoned and an outcast, through no fault of his own. This is so hard to bear. His physical sufferings are a trial in themselves; his loss of wealth, a major regret; and the treatment by his own relations, fellow-townsmen and the three friends, nearly impossible to bear. All of these are to him symptoms of his abandonment by God. It is all a personal dishonour for him. Why, why, has God done this to him? 'He has cast me into the mire, and I have become like dust and ashes' (30:19).

Again, we see Job partaking in the sufferings of Christ as he goes through all this. If we are suffering, let us remember that God does not reject us when we let off steam to him in prayer. He is bigger than that. He is more understanding and gracious than that. In fact, he loves to hear from us (Jer. 33:3). Our Father in heaven is happy if we talk to him and tell him what is on our heart and lay our sufferings before him at the throne of grace (Luke 11:2–4, 9–13; Heb. 4:16; Ps. 62:8).

Job believes that God sees all things (31:4). The fear of God in Job's heart leads him to respect all people, whether nobles, servants or foreigners—another reason why he is puzzled as to the lack of respect he is receiving from others! He has lived by the highest moral standards and God knows this. His personal righteousness produced holy living (31:1–4) and led to personal self-examination of the highest sort (31:5–40). His holiness is not ethereal or other-worldly, but practical, rooted in the soil of faith and watered by God's free grace.

This long section completes Job's speeches. However, we find Job still frustrated by his condition and the lack of answers to his questions. Thus, at the end of his lament we again discover Job's grace and high standard of morality. He has no more to ask and no more to say. He now rests in God's hands and trusts in his mercy. Throughout the monologue, Job has kept a high view of God and now leaves his prayers with him: 'Oh, that I had one to hear me! Here is my mark. Oh, that the Almighty would answer me ... The words of Job are ended' (31:35, 40b).

For further study ▶

FOR FURTHER STUDY

1. Make a study of 'wisdom' in the Old and New Testaments.

2. Study the statements in Job 26:7 and 10. How could Job have known that the earth hangs on nothing? What are the implications of believing the account of creation in the Bible?

3. Study Proverbs 8:27; Isaiah 40:22. How did these Old Testament writers know that the earth is a sphere? What are the implications regarding the authority of Scripture?

TO THINK ABOUT AND DISCUSS

1. People are very good at judging their neighbours and accusing them unjustly, just as these so-called friends of Job did, while not seeing the log in their own eye (Matt. 7:4). How can we be better than them?

2. How do you respond when God does not answer your prayers in the way you would like? How should you respond? Is your answer biblical?

3. 'Whatever you want men to do to you, do also to them' (Matt. 7:12). Job was not given this dignity. Why not?

10 Job's young friend

(32:1–38:2)

The conversation between Job and his three friends has come to an end. It would have been Zophar's turn to speak, but he chooses not to do so.

B
efore we consider God's words to Job, we need briefly to say something about chapters 32–38 and Elihu the young pretender, as he is something of an enigma. His name means 'he is my God', and he is to be identified with the kin of Abraham.[1] Several small commentaries and Bible studies on the Book of Job omit these chapters.[2] There are those who regard Elihu as a man led by the Spirit of God, while others are not so sure about this.[3] John E. Hartley tells us that Elihu was brought up well and had been taught in the ways of God and that his theological understanding is clearly seen in his four speeches. Many Bible students see Elihu as a picture type of Christ, as he seems the perfect bridge between Job's friends' analysis of his situation and the solution of the Lord. In short, he is a middleman between Job and God; a mediator to prepare for

God's coming on the scene. Other commentators, however, have less favourable views of Elihu, viewing him as garrulous and conceited.[4]

Elihu's anger (32:1–22)

The opening verses of this chapter give us an insight into the attitude and character of Elihu. Verses 1–10 emphasize straight away his anger towards both Job and his three friends. 'If you have understanding, hear this; listen to the sound of my words' (34:16).

His lengthy monologue—which is both a cross-examination of Job and a reaction to Job's dialogues with the friends—includes several ideas and allegations that have already been raised by the others against Job, so Elihu does not live up to his intention not to use their ideas (v. 14).

The word 'wrath' is found four times in the opening verses (vv. 2, 3, 5). Elihu is angry because of what both Job and his friends have been saying. Like the other friends, Elihu thinks that Job has justified himself during his contributions in the ongoing debate. He became incensed with Job for justifying himself rather than God (v. 2), and with the three friends for failing to answer Job adequately.

In his speech he summarizes twenty-nine chapters of discussion and blames Job's critics for not coming up with convincing arguments. He claims that he is only saying something now because of the failure of the other three to set Job straight. His words are not unlike those of the others, except that they claim to be unbiased, wiser, and therefore more helpful and instructive: 'Let me not, I pray, show partiality to anyone; nor let me flatter any man, for I do not know how to flatter, else my Maker would soon take me away' (vv. 21–22).

Elihu's self-confidence (33:1–37:24)

Without invitation, Elihu sets himself up as the mediator whom Job has so longed for: 'Truly I am as your spokesman before God; I also have been formed out of clay. Surely no fear of me will terrify you, nor will my hand be heavy on you' (33:6–7).

Elihu asserts that Job has said, 'I am pure, without transgression; I am innocent, and there is no iniquity in me'(33:9), yet there is no record of this in Job's words. He assumes that Job's pain and illness are sent to chasten him: 'Man is also chastened with pain on his bed, and with strong pain in many of his bones, so that his life abhors bread, and his soul succulent food' (33:19–20). We are wise to ask God to sanctify our troubles to us for holiness' sake and the glory of Christ (see Heb. 12).

> We are wise to ask God to sanctify our troubles to us for holiness' sake and the glory of Christ.

In chapter 34 Elihu turns his attention to the three friends (34:2–4), while continuing to slander Job (34:5–37:24). Can this be a true friend? The rest of his speech is a proud monologue seeking personal glory (34:10, 16, 34; 35:4; 36:2; 37:14).

Elihu's Judge (38:1–2)

Then the LORD answered Job out of the whirlwind, and said:
'Who is this who darkens counsel
By words without knowledge?'

Who is God speaking about—Elihu, Job, or both?—when he asks this question? Who is it that lacks understanding? It must be Elihu. This is because, firstly, God speaks immediately after Elihu, who has been articulate and bold (chs 32–37). However, his speech was provoked by anger and impatience (32:1–5, 9). Secondly, he claims to be respectful towards his elders, yet fails to speak in a respectful way to a renowned leader such as Job (32:6–14; 34:2; 42:7–8). We must remember that God does not impute to Job the sins which Elihu does. Thirdly, Elihu is compelled by his desire to share his opinion:

> I also will answer my part,
> I too will declare my opinion.
> For I am full of words;
> The spirit within me compels me.
> Indeed my belly is like wine that has no vent;
> It is ready to burst like new wineskins.
> I will speak, that I may find relief;
> I must open my lips and answer.

32:17–20

The personal pronouns 'I' and 'my' appear nine times in these words, demonstrating pride and overstated self-confidence. It is surely recorded this way to give emphasis and understanding regarding his attitude and true feelings.

Fourthly, Elihu fails miserably to bring any comfort to Job as either a bereaved man or a person suffering from acute illness. He is cold and utterly insensitive to Job's plight. There is no sympathy shown. As a result, Job has no questions for him. This is very telling. Fifthly, Elihu is utterly convinced that he is theologically correct, while boasting impartiality

(32:21–22). The author of the Book of Job makes no mistake and adds no spin. He is writing under the leading of the Holy Spirit, we believe (2 Peter 1:20–21).

For these reasons we must conclude that the Lord's words in 38:2 are about Elihu. If we say, however, that they are referring to Job, we would also need to say that the young Elihu is wiser than Job (this is, of course, always a possibility). Yet although Elihu listened well, he is not commended for his righteousness, nor his wisdom; nor had he been tried and attacked by Satan as Job; yet some commentators are quick to lay these words (38:2) at Job's door and to commend Elihu for his greater insights. Can this be correct? Can it be true that Job darkened the counsel of the Lord? In fact, Job spoke well when he spoke of Almighty God: 'you have not spoken of Me what is right, as My servant Job has' (42:7–8).

For these reasons we must not lay the words of 38:2 to Job's tally of errors. Elihu's anger is troubling: it is emphasized four times in 32:1–5. Several commentators pass over his anger lightly, but can this be welcomed? The Hebrew root of the word translated 'wrath' (*anaph*) indicates that it was seen in his face and heard in his breathing. It was a strong and powerful emotion. He was not merely angry, but very angry. If God commended Job and was happy with him (42:7, as quoted above), why was Elihu angry with Job at all? Surely there were no grounds for this reaction, and therefore his wrath was unwarranted!

Elihu's companions

When thinking about Job's friends—Eliphaz the Temanite, Bildad the Shuhite and Zophar the Naamathite—let us remember that their theological outlook is embraced still today by many Christians, Jews and Muslims when they insist that good deeds must surpass bad deeds in order for us to escape hell and to receive a favourable eternal destiny. This common mistake sets itself against the gospel of free grace found in the Scriptures. It was spoken against by John the Baptist and Jesus Christ (Matt. 3:9; 5:20), preached against by Paul (Eph. 2:8–9), and rejected by Martin Luther and other evangelical leaders at the time of the Protestant Reformation on the basis of Romans 1:16–17. It totally ignores the necessity of coming to God through Jesus Christ alone (John 14:6).

It is also necessary to note that:

- Job and his friends do not see eye to eye regarding the issue of suffering.
- Job and the three all think that they are right in this debate.
- Job and the three believe in the transcendence and omnipotence of Almighty God.
- Job and the three accept that all men and women will be judged by God.
- The friends lack a true understanding of the grace of God.

From this we can learn:

- The importance of correct theology and Bible knowledge when counselling and directing others. This is more important than experience. Empathy is always helpful, but theology correctly applied is the key to the best comfort and sympathy (2 Cor. 1:4–7; 4:1–6). This is also true with regard to church leadership. Without holy men schooled in the Scriptures of truth and grace, the churches will lack wise biblical guidance (2 Tim. 3).

- Job does not reject the sense of the transcendence or the omnipotence of God that the three have stressed; however, their lack of knowledge of God's grace and their inability to understand God's ways with his people is clear. This is because the three believe in a God who is to be feared, not in One who is to be loved (Luke 10:27).

- People often quote the three friends in sermons and literature, thinking them to be sound in theology and full of understanding of free grace, but this is not so. We must order our knowledge of them by God's remarks later on (42:7). They are not believers in the truest sense. They are theists, yes, but they are not regenerate children of God.

- We must remember that God did forgive the three when they repented and in faith accepted the atoning blood of sacrifice (42:8–9), as we will see later. In this, Job is a type of Christ: his sacrifice and prayers are accepted by the Father on behalf of lost souls (Eph. 5:2; Heb. 7:25). Because of Job, God showed them mercy.

For further study ▶

FOR FURTHER STUDY

1. What is regeneration and what are its fruits? Give examples from Scripture to support your answer.

2. Compare the grace of the Holy Spirit with the gifts of the Holy Spirit. What are their differences and their similarities?

3. Why do you think Elihu appears in the story of Job at all?

4. Study Genesis 4:5–6; Numbers 16:15; 2 Samuel 6:8; Jonah 4:4; Matthew 2:16–18; Ephesians 4:26. What are the fruits (consequences) of human anger?

TO THINK ABOUT AND DISCUSS

1. Why was God prepared to forgive Job's so-called friends? Does this encourage you?

2. How can we kill our anger? Is it as easy as 'counting up to ten'?

3. How can we make sure that we really and truly know God in Christ as our Saviour (see 2 Peter 1:5–11)?

11 God's famous words

(38:1–40:14)

We have come to the end of Job's dialogue with his friends and now find God speaking to Job. There is a tendency to think that the Book of Job is about Job or his friends; however, this is wrong. The Book of Job is all about God.

It is of course full of help regarding the question of personal suffering and the need for true faith in times of tragedy, as we have clearly seen. Yet it majors on the character and grace of Almighty God, Job's Saviour. God answers him over the course of two speeches (38:2–40:2 and 40:6–41:34), each one followed by a brief response from Job (40:3–5 and 42:1–6). Job's trials and sufferings now come into divine perspective. These famous chapters are of great interest, not only because here we have the words of God and their application to Job's individual sufferings—and, by extension, to all people of God—but also because they contain answers and implications regarding the question of creation in six days.

In an earlier chapter Job expressed the desire for God to speak to him: 'Oh, that I had one to hear me! Here is my mark. Oh, that the Almighty would answer me …!' (31:35). Job has been looking for answers and he wants God to justify his treatment of him. Previously Job had said,

Then call, and I will answer;

Or let me speak, then You respond to me.

How many are my iniquities and sins?

Make me know my transgression and my sin.

Why do You hide Your face,

And regard me as Your enemy?

13:22–24

When God's people feel that times are tough, pain is unbearable and bereavement is intolerable, then, as with Job, it affects their faith in a loving God. Such people need to learn from the Book of Job that there *is* hope for the journey. Job's quest for peace is not found in answers from God but in fellowship with God himself (1 John 1:3). God now steps in and fulfils Job's longings, but it does not have the outcome he imagined!

> Job's quest for peace is not found in answers from God but in fellowship with God himself.

God speaks (38:1–40:2)

Then the LORD answered Job out of the whirlwind …

38:1

Job was full of questions, but now God questions him and asks what Job cannot answer, regarding the creation of the world with its ecosystems, diversity of animals and governance: 'Now prepare yourself like a man; I will question you, and you shall answer Me' (38:3).

God's personal revelation, which we call a theophany (that is, the appearance of God to man), overwhelms Job. However, Job's reaction is, on one level, no real surprise and is a familiar response to the manifestation of God to men in whatever form it is given (Isa. 6:5; Dan. 10:10; see also Ezek. 1:28; Rev. 1:17).

The God of creation

Where were you when I laid the foundations of the earth?
Tell Me, if you have understanding.
Who determined its measurements?
Surely you know!
Or who stretched the line upon it?
To what were its foundations fastened?
Or who laid its cornerstone
When the morning stars sang together,
And all the sons of God shouted for joy?

38:4–7

God speaks of a supernaturally created universe which shows glimpses of his majesty, glory, wisdom and power. Thus, the main message for Job is that God as Creator rules by his eternal, sovereign, powerful and wise decrees. He instructs nature and sets up the order and governance of the cosmos (38:12, 31–33). He controls the elements and he created the beasts of the field, the goat, donkey, ox, ostrich, horse, hawk and eagle (39:1, 5, 9, 13, 19, 26–27). Government and providence belong to him. God concludes this first speech by saying, 'Shall the one who contends with the Almighty correct Him? He who rebukes God, let him answer it' (40:1–2).

In other words, 'How can *you* say that I am mismanaging my world? How can *you* accuse me of such error?' God rebukes Job; however, he wants Job to continue to place his hope in him. We have already noted that the God and Father of our Lord Jesus Christ is the 'God of hope' (Rom. 15:13). Since God is the Author of our salvation, Job can also call him 'the God of hope', for faith in God has given him eternal hope.

The God of light

> Where is the way to the dwelling of light?
> And darkness, where is its place …?
> By what way is light diffused?
>
> 38:19, 24

These are scientific questions. Henry Morris maintains, 'Light is not to be located in a certain place or situation. Neither does it simply appear or disappear, instantaneously. Light is travelling! It dwells in a "way", always on the way to some place … when light stops traveling, there is darkness. Thus darkness is static, staying in a place: but light is dynamic, dwelling in a way.'[1] Job did not answer this rhetorical question, but here is another indication of the fact that the ancients had a greater understanding of science than we give them credit for.

Job meets God (40:3–5)

> Then Job answered the LORD and said:
> 'Behold, I am vile;

What shall I answer You?

I lay my hand over my mouth. Once I have spoken, but I will
not answer;

Yes, twice, but I will proceed no further'

40:3–5

The revelation that the uncreated and eternal Creator God is
sovereign and rules as Lord over his creation seems so basic
and so obvious, but it was just what Job needed to bring him
a sense of fuller comprehension. He is now so overwhelmed
with God's sovereign majesty that he becomes aware of his
own insignificance: 'I am vile' (literally 'small'). He now
defers to God: 'What shall I answer You? I lay my hand over
my mouth' (v. 4).

Job stops himself from speaking by placing his hand over
his mouth. This illustrates the shock he has received through
understanding what God is and what God is getting at with
his questions.[2] He realizes that God cannot be argued with.
Now he has the opportunity to talk to God, he is gripped by
awe and is humbled in God's presence.

When God speaks, Job is silent! As a result, Job becomes
humble, happy and healthy again. It is pertinent to note:

- The Scriptures of the Old and New Testaments
  are to be read carefully, and readers must respond
  to God's precepts and promises with faith and
  repentance in the fear of God and with the help of
  the Holy Spirit.
- The fallen mind of man is not sufficient to find God.
  We need to hear God's voice through the Holy
  Scriptures of truth under the influence of the Holy
  Spirit (John 16:8). Job had understood the voice of

creation as it revealed a sovereign Designer, but he also needed to understand the words of God in order to have fellowship with him (John 1:1–3; 14:6).

- Never think that anyone will be proud or strong enough to be assertive in the presence of God on Judgement Day. People may be tempted to speak plainly and unreservedly now; they may shout at God when greatly distressed or in pain; but this will not be the case when they stand before him on the last day (Rev. 6:12–17).

- The doctrine of the sovereignty of God (Matt. 20:16; Rom. 9:13; Eph. 1:4–6) is one of the most neglected truths among Christians today. Yet understanding this truth properly is the door to salvation and to finding the fullness of peace and joy. When Job grasped this doctrine and its implications, he quickly began his road to recovery.

Job was mistaken

Job's questions 'Why me?' and 'Why now?' were mistakes. They were born of spiritual immaturity. Job now sees that he was mistaken:

- To doubt God. Job was wrong to doubt God's greatness, sovereignty, wisdom, and love for his creation and people. He now sees the bigger picture and a 'bigger' Saviour/Redeemer.

- To judge God. Job was wrong to set the fallen mind of man against the ways of a holy, just and righteous God. It is terribly wrong to think that man can fully understand God; it is foolish in the extreme. God is incomprehensible in his being. Zophar understood this: 'Can you search out the deep things of God? Can you find out the limits of the Almighty?' (11:7–8).

- To expect an easy life in a fallen world. The prince of this world still goes about like a 'roaring lion, seeking whom he may devour' (1 Peter 5:8). Satan was the tempter and enemy of Adam and Eve, and he is still our defeated accuser today (Gen. 3; Rev. 12:10). The devil opposed Jesus Christ in the wilderness and he still opposes the people of God (Matt. 4:1–11).

- To think that he would escape the trouble (tribulation) that all the redeemed of the Lord are destined to go through. It is necessary to take to heart these words of the Redeemer: 'These things I have spoken to you, that in Me you may have peace. In the world you will have tribulation; but be of good cheer, I have overcome the world' (John 16:33). The people of God must put on daily the whole armour of God (Eph. 6:10–20) and walk by faith, knowing that in this world they will experience trials.

- To want to avoid sharing in the sufferings of Christ. Suffering was Job's birthright as one of the redeemed children of the Lord. To suffer reproach, rejection, hostility, hatred and so on flows from the Christian's identification with Christ and his church; it is therefore not to be loathed, for the Saviour has said, 'Blessed are those who are persecuted for righteousness' sake, for theirs is the kingdom of heaven. Blessed are you when they revile and persecute you, and say all kinds of evil

against you falsely for My sake. Rejoice and be
exceedingly glad, for great is your reward in heaven,
for so they persecuted the prophets who were before
you' (Matt. 5:10–12). Paul could see good emerging
from both his afflictions and his comfort. Both were
sanctified to him by the cross (2 Cor. 1:3–7).

Charles H. Spurgeon's words are once again helpful at this
point:

There are great benefits to come out of these severe trials and
depressions. You cannot make great soldiers without war, or
train skillful seamen upon shore. It appears necessary that, if
a man is to become a great believer, he must be greatly tried;
if he is to be a great helper of others, he must pass through
the temptations of others; if he is to be greatly instructed
in the things of the kingdom, he must learn by experience;
and if he is to be a loud singer to the tune of sovereign grace,
he must hear deep calling unto deep at the noise of God's
waterspouts. The uncut diamond has but little brilliance, the
unthreshed corn feeds none, and so the untried professor is of
small practical use or beauty. The time shall come with you
whose faces are covered with sorrow, when you shall bless
God for your sorrows; the day will come when you shall set
much store by your losses and your crosses, your troubles and
your afflictions, counting them happy which endure.[3]

The people of God are not to think that God owes them
an easy life because they are good, obedient and his beloved,
adopted children. Nonetheless, he has promised never to
leave them nor forsake them (Ps. 23:1; Heb. 13:5–6; 1 Peter
5:7). Surely these promises are to be treasured and grasped
during our short pilgrimage here below?

God and Job (40:6–14)

Job had been right to maintain his innocence in the face of his friends' false accusations (see 42:7–8), but he was foolish, so God says, 'Now prepare yourself like a man; I will question you, and you shall answer Me; would you indeed annul My judgment? Would you condemn Me that you may be justified?' (vv. 7–8).

By these words, we learn that Job's attitude all along has been one of taking God for granted, as if Job was made for God's benefit. Job has felt all along that God has dealt unjustly with him and that God's governance of the world was somehow faulty and verging on the unjust. Now God asks, 'Who is right Job—you or me?' It is one thing to trust in the righteousness that is imputed to sinners by faith alone for salvation, but quite another to trust in one's own righteous deeds for peace with God. Job made this mistake. The former is fully and happily accepted by God for ever when faith is present (Rom. 5:1), while the latter is always tainted by indwelling sin, a lack of assurance and false assumptions needing correction. This is a lesson that always needs relearning. Once justified by faith (alone), the Lord's saints are not to try to be right with God by works of righteousness. It is true that the people of God are to be zealous to do and maintain good works, but not for justification; instead out of love and duty

> Once justified by faith (alone), the Lord's saints are not to try to be right with God by works of righteousness.

as the servants of Jesus Christ (Titus 2:14; 3:14). Through his complaints, Job gave the impression that he was trusting in his own righteousness. This is what his friends and Elihu thought, but they were mistaken. Perhaps this was so because they were not right with God themselves (Phil. 3:9–11; Titus 3:5). What Job needed to recognize and understand was God's purposes for him as *his* child, God's plans for *him* and God's work in *him*. Job was also to realize that he could not know more than God, nor did he have the power to rule the world or humble the proud. Job was not able to adorn himself with splendour or majesty, so how could he possibly govern a world so needy of attention? The Old Testament speaks of God's 'marvelous lovingkindness' (Ps. 17:7), while the New Testament shows us that God is longsuffering and will give time for repentance and faith to be seen in the hearts of sinners (2 Peter 3:9).

Job's mandate

... prepare yourself like a man.

v. 7a

There are God-designed biological and psychological differences between male and female, created on the sixth day (Gen. 1:26). God expects men to be men, saved by free and sovereign grace, and they will be judged as made in his image. God sees gender differences clearly when it comes to male and female roles in his ordered universe. Sin has tended to mar the contrasts between the sexes as created by God. Rejection of God's will in this matter, as set out in his Word, is eating away in society at the definitive order set by God in the hearts of those made in his image in the beginning. The theory of evolution, which is used by feminists and others to support change in the God-ordained roles of men and women, has had disastrous moral and social consequences in society. The New Testament is, however, clear with regard to God's created order (Col. 3:18–4:1).[4]

For further study ▶

FOR FURTHER STUDY

1. What are the fruits of the believer's mystical union with Jesus Christ in redemption?

2. What do the following portions of the New Testament tell us about Christian suffering: Romans 8:14–18; 2 Corinthians 4:4–12; James 1:2; 1 Peter 1:6–7?

3. Read Isaiah 43:1; 66:1; Daniel 4:35; Romans 8:29–30; 9:3, 11–13; Ephesians 1:5, 11. What do these passages teach about God's sovereignty?

TO THINK ABOUT AND DISCUSS

1. Job wondered, 'Why me?' and looked for an answer. He asked this question as if he alone was to be spared the consequences of sin, and the refiner's fire, while others were to suffer. Did he get an answer?

2. Can you say, 'I know the "fellowship of Christ's sufferings"'? How would you explain to your friends what this means?

3. 'Behold, I am vile; what shall I answer You? I lay my hand over my mouth. Once I have spoken, but I will not answer; yes, twice, but I will proceed no further' (Job 40:4–5). This was Job's reaction to God's words in chapters 38–39. How ought we to react to Christ's voice in the Scriptures and providence?

12 God's great creatures

(40:15–42:6)

The two great creatures in this section—the behemoth and Leviathan—are used by God to press upon Job that he (God) is the almighty sovereign Lord of creation and he will do as he pleases. This is, of course, what Job knows, but he had not grasped that his understanding was incomplete and that his previous conclusions were not up to the mark.

Two great creatures (40:15–41:34)

The behemoth (40:15–24)

> Look now at the behemoth, which I made along with you;
> He eats grass like an ox.
> See now, his strength is in his hips,
> And his power is in his stomach muscles.
> He moves his tail like a cedar;
> The sinews of his thighs are tightly knit.

His bones are like beams of bronze,
His ribs like bars of iron.

vv. 15–18

'Behemoth' is the transliteration of the plural of the Hebrew word for 'beast' and is here used as a proper noun. Many commentators are utterly perplexed by the description and blame it on exaggerations and the many obscurities in the text. They suggest that the hippopotamus fits the text best. Francis I. Andersen notes, 'The despair of all commentators, the innumerable conflicting solutions offered, do not encourage us to accept any of them.'[1] However, God has not left us in complete darkness as to what the behemoth was. If we accept that the description of this immense animal is God-given, it fits the profile of a dinosaur. No living animal fits this description, so we must look to those creatures that are now extinct. Those who accept the long ages of evolutionary geology opt for a hippopotamus or a rhinoceros. However, the text cries out for something like a large sauropod dinosaur (*Brachiosaurus*) with a powerful body and a large and long tail. Failure to accept the text as inspired leads to making the mistake of rejecting the Bible as true in fact as well as in doctrine. Its interpretation may be difficult for some, but the Word of God cannot lie (Titus 1:2).

Thus we see that, in Job's day, people were still familiar with this creature. The Bible hereby gives us clear evidence that dinosaurs and people really did live together. 'Look now at the behemoth, which I made along with you' (v. 15).[2]

Should we accept the description of the behemoth as a myth? Not if we believe verse 19: 'He is the first of the ways of God; only He who made him can bring near His sword.' This verse calls for special attention as it points to a mighty creature. It accords the behemoth the place of honour as 'the first of the ways ['works', AV and ESV] of God'. It was the crown of the animal creation or the first beast created on day six of creation week (Gen. 1:24–25), being the largest of all the land animals.[3]

Leviathan (41:1–34)

'Leviathan' is a transliteration of a Hebrew word that literally means 'twisted animal'. The Septuagint rendered this 'the dragon'.[4] Many commentators say that Leviathan must be a crocodile, while the New English Bible has settled for a whale. It is clear from the text that it had a violent disposition; it was unconquerable and very fierce. It is legitimate to see Leviathan as a terrifying serpentine sea creature (a *Kronosaurus*, perhaps).[5] The Bible says that it was covered by a spear-proof scaly armour (vv. 15–17, 23, 26–30), was incredibly fierce (vv. 8–10, 25, 33) and powerful (v. 12), and was able to breathe fire: 'Out of his mouth go burning lights; sparks of fire shoot out. Smoke goes out of his nostrils, as from a boiling pot and burning rushes. His breath kindles coals, and a flame goes out of his mouth' (vv. 19–21).

This creature has already appeared in Job, at 3:8: 'May those curse it [the day of Job's birth] who curse the day, those who are ready to arouse Leviathan.'

Here is a poetic description of a well-known formidable beast in Job's day. The text does not suggest that Leviathan is a mythological monster. Job 41:1 begins a string of questions with God aiming to convince Job that he is helpless in the presence of such a frightening creature—how could you catch or even kill him? Moreover, even if you could do that, what would you then do with him? Verses 9–11 dwell on the folly of tackling him, and the rest of the chapter is devoted to a detailed description of the creature (vv. 12–34). Some commentators do not take the text seriously: 'Space does not permit detailed commentary on all the whimsical things that the Lord says about Leviathan. Our poet can hardly write a line without including a simile, a habit which many critics censure as artistic over-kill.'[6] However, there is a problem with this approach: no one except perhaps a child is afraid of a fictional or mythical creature. Yet the argument in the text is that Job is unable to stand and do battle with Leviathan; therefore how can he stand before God? This is God's point, and for it to be valid, Leviathan needs to be real and a very scary, powerful beast.[7] 'No one is so fierce that he would dare stir him up. Who then is able to stand against Me? Who has preceded Me, that I should pay him? Everything under heaven is Mine' (vv. 10–11).

> Job is unable to stand and do battle with Leviathan; therefore how can he stand before God?

As in the case of the behemoth, God does not describe any animal known to us today. We must again look to those creatures that lived before and after the flood and are now extinct. It is also necessary to note that by the time the description is complete, Leviathan has become a fire-breathing dragon, a satanic symbol of chaos, evil and destruction (v. 34).

Leviathan appears another three times in the Old Testament, in connection with:

- The creation event: 'This great and wide sea, in which are innumerable teeming things, living things both small and great. There the ships sail about; there is that Leviathan which You have made to play there' (Ps. 104:25–26).
- The exodus event, when God delivered his people from Egypt: 'For God is my King from of old, working salvation in the midst of the earth. You divided the sea by Your strength; You broke the heads of the sea serpents in the waters. You broke the heads of Leviathan in pieces and gave him as food to the people inhabiting the wilderness' (Ps. 74:12–14).
- The Judgement Day event—God defeating Leviathan at the end of time: 'In that day the LORD with His severe sword, great and strong, will punish Leviathan the fleeing serpent, Leviathan that twisted serpent; and He will slay the reptile that is in the sea' (Isa. 27:1). God alone can overcome it, and he will do so with his sword (Job 40:19).

Leviathan is a 'piercing' and 'crooked' serpent called 'the dragon' (Isa. 27:1, KJV).[8] It is evident that the Old Testament sees this creature as a type of antichrist or Satan who will be defeated at the second advent of our Lord Jesus Christ. In the Book of Revelation, a great, fiery red dragon, Satan, is cast out of heaven (Rev. 12). It is an image of the enemy of the people of God. Calvin 'supposes ... that under this image other enemies of the church are embraced, and does not doubt that *allegorically* Satan and his kingdom are intended'.[9] Only God can control and destroy Leviathan, and Job can only shrink back in humble fear of this creature. By means of rhetorical questions, the Lord demonstrates Job's inability to confront, much less subdue, this great creature.

Job's reflection (42:1–6)

Job's reflection on God's words has made him acknowledge God's sovereign power: 'I know that You can do everything, and that no purpose of Yours can be withheld from You' (v. 2).

He admits that God is wise and that all he does and allows is within the framework of his divine sovereignty, wisdom and love. Job also confesses that he is not capable of fully understanding all the ways of God—they are too extraordinary for him. Having understood God's intervention and meaning, Job now realizes that he has failed in knowledge and lacked humility. The behemoth and Leviathan are not able to be controlled by Job, so he is in no position to judge God's rule of *his* universe. Again, Job must defer to God and acknowledge that he is King and Lord. Job must resort to his first instincts of faith uttered back in 1:22. Then he did not question God's love or justice. Now, he not only believes but also repents (v. 6), acknowledging that God is all-wise. He is not confessing sinfulness but poor judgement and lack of comprehension. If men and women would walk with God and know the communion of the Holy Spirit, they need to walk humbly in accordance with his will and in the light of life (Eph. 5:17; 1 John 1:7).

Job fears God

> I have uttered what I did not understand, things too wonderful for me, which I did not know.

v. 3

As Job reflects on God's words, he finds peace with God. His humility is seen in his acceptance of God's revelation to him and not, as some suppose, his admission that he is at fault. God looks for signs of humility and expects his people to humble themselves before him. It is a fault to ask God to humble us. If we ask this, he may very well do so—in a way that we will never forget! The children of God are commanded to humble themselves: 'Therefore humble yourselves under the mighty hand of God, that He may exalt you in due time, casting all your care upon Him, for He cares for you' (1 Peter 5:6–7).

For further study ▶

FOR FURTHER STUDY

1. Look up all the references to the behemoth in the Bible. Can we conclude that God created dinosaurs on day six of creation week (see Gen. 1:25)?

2. Look up all the references to Leviathan in the Bible. Do you think that the creature was real? Does it also represent a greater and more powerful force?

3. Can Hebrew poetry speak about real people and events, keeping true to the facts? Find other examples in the Old Testament of Hebrew poetry that tells of facts.

TO THINK ABOUT AND DISCUSS

1. Why would some commentators want to dismiss the idea that the behemoth and Leviathan were extinct dinosaur-type creatures?

2. Was it Job's fear of God or his sense of self-preservation that made him yield to God?

3. What is the true fear of God? How is it seen?

13 Job's vindication

(42:1–17)

The epilogue of this book is not, as some commentators suggest, a likely add-on to make a conclusion, nor is it a repositioned portion of prose taken from an older beginning to the Book of Job. Rather, it is an appropriate conclusion and a fitting revelation regarding the powerful work of renewal in the life of a believer.

We will see that 'Job died, old and full of days' (v. 17), and was dignified by God in the sight of his contemporaries. There is an indication of this in verses 7–8 when the phrase 'My servant Job' is used four times, clearly signifying God's acceptance of him. If we couple this with the use of the same wording at the beginning of the book (1:8; 2:3), we realize that the Job at the beginning of the book is the same Job at the end and is still as highly regarded. This ending of the book is not to be regarded as improbable. However, it makes us stop and ask what God is saying, given that 'All

Scripture is given by inspiration of God' (2 Tim. 3:16). This is the start of Job's public vindication.

Job's repentance (vv. 2–6)

> I have heard of You by the hearing of the ear,
> But now my eye sees You.
> Therefore I abhor myself,
> And repent in dust and ashes.
>
> vv. 5–6

As we saw at the end of the previous chapter, there has been a marked change in Job since God spoke to him personally. This is not surprising; in fact, it is normal in those who receive light and grace from the Word of God. They are like the dry bones in Ezekiel's vision which were resurrected and given new life on hearing the Word of the Lord (Ezek. 37:3–4). We see something similar with Paul before his conversion. He was a zealous enemy of the followers of Jesus Christ and he persecuted them, not thinking that he was sinning against God and Christ. Later, he admitted that he had been a 'blasphemer, a persecutor, and an insolent man' (1 Tim. 1:13)—but what a change in him after he heard the words of Jesus Christ on the Damascus road! Afterwards, he preached the message that 'the Christ would suffer, that He would be the first to rise from the dead, and would proclaim light to the Jewish people and to the Gentiles' (Acts 26:23).

When God speaks through his Word and by his Spirit, this change is typical. The heart is opened, the conscience cleansed, the mind illumined (Rom. 12:1–3) and the will freed. Job expresses this change in terms of repentance: 'Therefore I abhor myself, and repent in dust and ashes'

(42:6). This marked change in Job is brought about through reflecting on the words of God his Saviour.

But Job is righteous! So in what way does he repent? It is clear that, having reflected on the powerful words of God, he has realized that he spoke hastily: 'I have uttered what I did not understand, things too wonderful for me, which I did not know' (v. 3). He now renounces the foolish notion that *he* is more loving and just than God: 'I have heard of You by the hearing of the ear, but now my eye sees You' (v. 5). He shows godly sorrow: 'Therefore I abhor myself, and repent in dust and ashes' (v. 6). (The verb 'abhor' has no object in the original Hebrew; therefore, the phrase 'I abhor myself' could also read, 'I abhor my words' or 'I abhor my immaturity'.)

> The act of repentance is an ongoing affair in the life of the people of God, not just a one-time moment.

The act of repentance is an ongoing affair in the life of the people of God, not just a one-time moment. Day-after-day repentance is the fruit of evangelical faith which always looks to the cross and the atoning blood of Christ for cleansing. The person who is right with God (justified), as Job was, is not perfect, so God has provided the blood of Jesus Christ to go on cleansing from all sin in response to the confession of sin. To confess our sin is to agree with God about our personal guilt; such confession is found in a renewed contrite heart. In response to such confession God promises there will be constant cleansing and forgiveness from defilement (1 John 1:9). On believing, our debt is remitted by God and the stain of our sin is removed.

Feeling godly sorrow and striving for holiness is part of the Spirit's work in those who believe. Sanctification occurs at conversion and is the setting apart of believers unto Christ as his bride through their mystical union with him. Progressive sanctification is that ongoing spiritual work of grace whereby God refines, perfects and prepares the soul for heaven. The *Westminster Shorter Catechism* explains it thus: 'Sanctification is the work of God's free grace, whereby we are renewed in the whole man after the image of God, and are enabled more and more to die unto sin, and to live unto righteousness.'[1] The people of God are to cooperate in this process.

God's words to Job bring further changes into his life. While God had declared Job righteous (1:8; 2:3), Job still had progress to make in his faith. This is what God promises to achieve in all his redeemed people: 'The LORD will perfect that which concerns me' (Ps. 138:8; see also 1 Cor. 1:8; Eph. 5:25, 27; Phil. 1:6; 1 Thes. 5:23). Through his trials and pains, Job found what the renewed inner person longs for: a clearer view of God and deeper fellowship with him through the fellowship of Christ's suffering. How often have Christians asked God to draw closer to them, only to complain when it involves the kinds of trials Job experienced! Job has now what he could not have known except in fellowship with Christ: 'I have heard of You by the hearing of the ear, but now my eye sees You' (v. 5).

Christians can and do suffer because of their mystical union with the Lord Jesus Christ. This is something God's people should be happy about, because all that the true people of God endure when on earth comes to them in fellowship with their Saviour. It is not possible to live a godly life and not share the fellowship of Christ's sufferings (2 Tim. 3:12). This is God's plan for his people, and being in Christ makes it inevitable and glorious (Phil. 3:10).

Job's restoration (vv. 7–11)

Job has been vindicated, his fortune restored twice over (v. 10) and his life extended for another 140 years (v. 16). He will die after a long and blessed life, while his three friends are condemned but brought to repentance through the witness of Job and the grace of God (vv. 8–9). What is happening here is in keeping with other portions of Scripture. What I describe as Job's realization (40:4–5), reflection (42:2–3) and repentance (42:5–6) have brought about spiritual renewal for Job. There are clear signs of his renewal:

New victory (v. 5)

Job overcame the trials set for him by Satan. Job never renounced God but remained true to his convictions. Ultimately, Job's friends were the tools of Satan, but they were also there to work as God's stonecutters, and God meant it for good. Job's victory came by the power of God through faith (1 Peter 1:5). What's more, Satan worked through unbelief and false teaching (theology).

New energy (v. 17)

Job had been very ill, but now his physical weakness and

pains are gone. New health to the soul is accompanied by the healing of Job's body, resulting in a new zeal for spiritual things: 'Job died, old and full of days' (v. 17). This renewing power of God is seen in the New Testament account of the woman who had been ill for twelve years. When she came to the Saviour and by faith touched the hem of Christ's garment, he said that he 'perceived power going out from Me' (Luke 8:46). The woman knew an instant change for the better. Job's repentance and faith (for they always go together) were the 'hands' that reached out to God, and the result was that soul and body were supplied with renewed vitality.

New spiritual authority (vv. 8–10)

Job was able to forgive others. A new forgiving spirit was granted him. 'And the LORD restored Job's losses when he prayed for his friends' (v. 10). In forgiving, we are forgiven (Luke 6:38). God said, 'My servant Job shall pray for you. For I will accept him' (v. 8). Power in prayer returns to Job and to all who forgive others their trespasses against themselves. Job's prayers for his friends are accepted: 'the LORD had accepted Job' (v. 9). Intercessory prayer is a Holy Spirit-urged ministry and is seen in those led by the Spirit (Eph. 6:18). Our willingness to forgive is proof that we ourselves have been forgiven (Matt. 6:14–15; 18:21–22), while 'The effective prayer of a righteous man to turn away God's

> Power in prayer returns to Job and to all who forgive others their trespasses against themselves.

anger from the wicked (cf. Gen. 18) adds another meaning to Job's suffering that no one had thought of'.[2]

New peace in the soul (vv. 10–11)

Job had been ridiculed, called a liar and rejected, nevertheless he prays for all his detractors now: 'My servant Job shall pray for you. For I will accept him' (v. 8). He is assured of God's vindication before his friends. Job was bankrupt, but now he will work again for a living. Job was able to forgive those who opposed him and to hold no bitterness or bear any grudges towards them (v. 10). Job stands as a mediator—something he had thought about, but he never imagined this role for himself. Here we see Job's priestly office, and we are reminded of the Protestant doctrine of the priesthood of all believers. His desire was for someone to mediate between him and God (Jehovah). Now he is the priest, and his accusers are the recipients of God's grace: 'he prayed for his friends' (v. 10). This is a clear picture of the gospel: of Jesus Christ, the only Mediator between God and man, who ever lives to make intercession for the sins of his people by continuously presenting the blood of his sacrifice to the Father for propitiation (Rom. 8:34). God granting double blessings (vv. 8, 10, 12) speaks of his *joy* in Job and his rejoicing over his restoration.

Restored relationships (v. 11)

Brothers, sisters and close friends consoled and comforted Job (v. 11). They helped him by bringing gifts. This is God at work, and a minor miracle. Where were these relatives when he was very ill? Perhaps they were afraid to help, thinking that Job was under God's judgement. Thus they kept their distance and withheld their support until it was clear that he was innocent of the charges his three friends were making. Some friends are fair-weather friends like these. These brothers, sisters and other close acquaintances had a change of heart when it became clear that God had not abandoned Job or rejected him. When trouble hits, it is always good to get support from friends who will console, understand and provide comfort. Job's vertical relationship was renewed and restored, and good horizontal relations followed as a result.

New joy (v. 10–17)

Job is now thankful for his sufferings! 'And the LORD restored Job's losses when he prayed for his friends. Indeed the LORD gave Job twice as much as he had before' (v. 10). God doubled his former blessings to make it clear that he was honouring Job (v. 12). This was necessary because it was the common wisdom of the time that the wealthy were the recipients of God's special favour. Job was receiving recognition for believing perseverance (James 5:7). His new children were a reward from God (Ps. 127:3). The name Jemimah speaks of dove-like qualities. Keziah—from Cassia, a variety of cinnamon—represents charm and fragrance. Keren-Happuch, a black powder used to decorate the eyes, points to attractiveness. His daughters were famous for their beauty (v. 15).

Job's commendation (vv. 12–17)

These verses are God's concluding remarks and we must take heed to them when interpreting the whole message of the Book of Job. God's view of Job, of his friends and of the events recorded are definitive, and his response must be our response. In my exposition of these chapters I have tried to interpret the text in a way that reflects God's mind in all matters. Job had rejected his friends' philosophical and doctrinal position, as well as their unhelpful approach to his personal sufferings. In this last chapter we find that God rejects their ideas too, and calls them to repentance (vv. 7–9).

God's anger

What makes God angry? It is clear from these verses that false witness, false teaching and poor doctrine are abhorrent to him. The three friends were not correct in their doctrine of God, but Job was. Job got his facts straight, while the others failed to speak well of God, even if it seemed otherwise in their speeches: 'the LORD said to Eliphaz the Temanite, "My wrath is aroused against you and your two friends, for you have not spoken of Me what is right, as My servant Job has' (v. 7).

This rebuke from God might seem strange, especially when we think of their 'insights' into God's nature and character throughout the debate, but God is clear: they were in error. We see, then, the importance of truth and the necessity of the study of theology for our church leaders. God has revealed himself in his creation and more perfectly and completely in the pages of Holy Scripture. We must not think that our fallen minds can know God without us knowing Jesus Christ his only Son and the work of the Holy Spirit in regeneration (1 Cor. 2:14; John 17:3).

152

God's servant

> My servant Job.

v. 8

As noted earlier, this phrase is used four times in this
portion, and two times in the early chapters of the book
(vv. 7–8; 1:8; 2:3), that is, six times in total! What God had
said at the beginning of Job's trials is repeated at the end
of all his troubles. Thus we see that God acknowledges
that Job remains righteous in his sight. The nature of
justification is such that once we have been declared
righteous in God's sight, it remains true for always, while
sanctification is an ongoing process not complete until
death. Job's relationship was a living and vital one which
was beyond dispute and could not be broken in spite of
what he had been through. The trial of his faith proved
him to be a genuine believer and man of God whose
prayers had power with God: 'My servant Job shall pray
for you. For I will accept him' (v. 8).

God's mercy

How can God be merciful? The Bible is clear: it is through
atoning sacrifice. God requires a sacrifice for the forgiveness
of sins. This is nothing new. It goes back to the first book
of the Bible and to the act of faith which Abel, the second
son of Adam and Eve, undertook to atone for his personal
sins: 'By faith Abel offered to God a more excellent sacrifice
than Cain, through which he obtained witness that he was
righteous, God testifying of his gifts; and through it he being
dead still speaks' (Heb. 11:4; see Gen. 4).

Sin offerings and burnt offerings were prescribed in the Old Testament for propitiation and the forgiveness of sins (Gen. 8:20; 22:13; Lev. 5:14–6:7). Job's friends were commanded to offer sacrifices as atonement for their sins. They were to bring 'seven bulls and seven rams' (v. 8). This was a sign of the seriousness of their folly. These men were rich: only the rich could afford this type of offering. Before God, all are sinners (Rom. 3:23), and he commands all people everywhere to repent (Matt. 3:2; Luke 13:3; Acts 3:19). The grace of God is seen here. The three, if they will obey and trust in the blood of the appointed sacrifice, will be forgiven their sins: 'He will even deliver one who is not innocent' (22:30a). The Old Testament holds true to this good news: 'when I see the blood, I will pass over you' (Exod. 12:13).

For further study ▶

FOR FURTHER STUDY

1. What are the fruits of repentance and godly sorrow? Give Scripture references to back up your answer.

2. Why is atoning sacrifice necessary for salvation? What makes it powerful and acceptable to God?

3. Study Job 42. What attributes (essential characteristics) of God do we see in this chapter?

TO THINK ABOUT AND DISCUSS

1. What are the marks of the Holy Spirit in a believer's life (Gal. 5:16–26)?

2. Reflect on John 16:24. What brings most joy to the believer?

3. Were the three friends deserving of God's mercy? Why did God command them to repent? What are the implications of this for yourself? For your non-Christian friends and family members?

14 Job's perseverance

(James 5:11)

James 5 is the only place in the New Testament where reference to Job is made: 'Indeed we count them blessed who endure. You have heard of the perseverance of Job and seen the end intended by the Lord—that the Lord is very compassionate and merciful' (5:11).

I t is sufficient for us to believe that Job was a real person and that the Book of Job is an accurate history of his life, times and spiritual trials. The apostle James speaks well of Job as a great man of God, saying, 'You have heard of the perseverance of Job.' This takes us back to the Book of Job to see his patience and pilgrimage under trial.

Job was patient in trial, and God said that his attitude was good, yes, very good. He was a man of God with a faith that held on to the end, and this New Testament verse honours him in this regard. In this introductory commentary we have seen his faith shine out of the darkness when death, heartbreak and humiliation were his portion. Job was clearly

God's servant, and the apostle James wants his readers to note Job's perseverance in faith.

Remembering Job's faith

Job's faith holds firm

> 'Naked I came from my mother's womb,
> And naked shall I return there.
> The LORD gave, and the LORD has taken away;
> Blessed be the name of the LORD.'
> In all this Job did not sin nor charge God with wrong.
>
> Job 1:21–22

What grace Job showed when utterly bereaved! He 'arose, tore his robe, and shaved his head'; then he 'fell to the ground and worshiped' (v. 20). His actions were due to his personal sense of the awe and majesty of Almighty God. Job accepted the hand of God's mysterious providence for him and his wife, and he retained immense dignity and the desire to worship and believe. Job accepted that the Lord was in control over all circumstances: 'Naked I came from my mother's womb, and naked shall I return there. The LORD gave, and the LORD has taken away.'

Faith in testing times

> Though He slay me, yet will I trust Him.
> Even so, I will defend my own ways before Him.
>
> Job 13:5

This verse is a powerful statement of Job's trust in God. Job is sure of his access to God (13:15b–16). Men and women are not saved because of our works of righteousness but through believing the truth about God and his plan of salvation (the gospel). Learning is vain unless it brings us to the knowledge of the truth as it is in Jesus Christ (Eccles. 1:2). Faith is knowledge that turns to conviction, and conviction, when it turns to trust, believes in Jesus Christ alone for forgiveness and justification. When repentant sinners are declared righteous in God's sight, they are forgiven all their sins, past, present and future. Job found grace in the eyes of God, and this shone through in his perseverance under trial. He thought like the psalmist after him, 'For You are my hope, O Lord GOD; You are my trust from my youth' (Ps. 71:5). The daily challenge of the people of God is to conquer their fears through trust in the promises of God and the gospel. No matter how hot the battle, the Christian knows that ultimate victory is sure: 'If God is for us, who can be against us?' (Rom. 8:31).

Faith has hope

> For I know that my Redeemer lives,
> And He shall stand at last on the earth;
> And after my skin is destroyed, this I know,
> That in my flesh I shall see God,
> Whom I shall see for myself,
> And my eyes shall behold, and not another.

Job 19:25–27

These are perhaps the most famous words of Job; here we find the faith of Job shining through despite all his troubles, pains and difficulties. His is the language of the believer. He is convinced that 'the sufferings of this present time are not worthy to be compared with the glory which shall be revealed

in us [i.e. the people of God]' (Rom. 8:18). He is convinced that
God is his Redeemer and that he will see God, whether in the
flesh or out of it; and when he does, God will be on his side: 'this
I know, that in my flesh I shall see God.' The testing of God's
people is part of the preparation and perfecting of Christ's
bride, the church. Just as the fellowship of his sufferings is
an indispensible and unavoidable part of believers' mystical
union with their Saviour, so the work of sanctification will lead
to their glorification. Job is being tested through the fires of
bereavement, prolonged illness and public shame, but he is
growing in grace because God, who has begun a good work
in him, will complete it, as he will do for all the true people
of God. This assures God's people that times of testing and
suffering are appointed and performed by God. Job was now
willing to accept that all his problems were the will of God for
him. Suffering is not pointless but planned by God for us.

Faith holds patience

> But He knows the way that I take;
> When He has tested me, I shall come forth as gold.
>
> Job 23:10

Job believes that God will 'perform what is appointed for me'
(23:14). This is about God's plan for his life. The covenant
of redemption promises a spotless bride for the Redeemer
(Rev. 21:2, 9). Job did not stop believing. Yes, he questioned
God's justice and sovereign providence; however, during his
trials he stopped praising and rejoicing only for a short while,
because his heartache and trials were a constant sorrow for
him. He did not move off the pathway the leads to life eternal,
nor did he, like Christian and Pilgrim in Bunyan's *Pilgrim's*

Progress, hop over the fence into By-path Meadow. He did not think that the grass was greener on the broad road of unbelief that leads to destruction, but rather was sure that 'When He has tested me, I shall come forth as gold' (23:10). The people of God are called to walk in faith and to cooperate with the Holy Spirit's leading and instruction through the Word of God. They are to live in the Spirit and walk in the Spirit, being led by him (Gal. 5:25, 18). 'Christ's work is not done with a soul when He has brought it to pardon—when He has washed it in His own Blood. Oh, no! The better half of salvation remains—His great work of sanctification remains.'[1] In the light of Job's faith, no wonder James writes, 'You have heard of the perseverance of Job and seen the end intended by the Lord—that the Lord is very compassionate and merciful' (5:11).

Considering Job's perseverance

> You have heard of the perseverance of Job.
>
> James 5:11b

Job's attitude through his trials was one of 'perseverance', which has regard to things and circumstances. It is contrasted by James with 'patience', which in the original Greek is a compound word (a variant of which is used four times in vv. 7–11), and which literally means 'long temper', hence 'longsuffering'. It emphasizes patience with regard to antagonistic people. James tells his readers that the prophets of the Old Testament were good examples of this grace. It is true that Job's three friends annoyed him, but although he was curt with them at times, Job was persevering and patient in his faith. Thinking of the distinction between the two words 'perseverance' and 'patience', 'perseverance' (*hupomone*) denotes 'to bear up courageously (under suffering)', while 'patience' (*makrothumia*) 'is that quality of self-restraint in the face of provocation which does not hastily retaliate'.[2]

Job shows God-given strength not to buckle under trial. Perseverance is necessary when we have no choice but to bear with the present trial. Job had no choice but to go through his illness and pain and to wait for God to intervene, undertake and answer prayer. Therefore, perseverance is 'Steadfast endurance, the virtue shown by martyrs'.[3]

Remembering Job's hope

> ... and seen the end intended by the Lord—that the Lord is very compassionate and merciful.
>
> James 5:11c

Job's trials produced in him a hope that does not disappoint (Ps. 119:116; Rom. 5:5). When Job could do nothing else, he fell back on the unchanging nature of God. The people of God must not let sufferings turn them to bitterness and doubt. They must build on the solid rock, on the promises of the Scriptures given to them as their birthright in Jesus Christ, and not on the shifting sands of unbelief and anger. Hearts must not be hardened or unbelief tolerated, as neither attitude expects or asks anything from God. Job found these hard to avoid, yet he knew that in due time God would help him (14:19; 17:15; 23:2; 27:2). His trials were intended to bring him closer to God.

The object of Job's hope

The object of Job's hope was God himself. Job exercised faith in the God who keeps his promises, so hope settled in his heart. This certain expectation was a product of his faith and because of God's mercy. The people of God are promised that Christ will never, ever leave them or forsake them (Titus 1:2; Heb. 13:5; 1 Peter 5:7; Jude 24–25). This is why Paul says in 2 Timothy 2:13, 'He remains faithful'—that is, to his holy character and gracious promises.

The comfort and encouragement of Job's hope

Christian hope, according to Hebrews 6:18, is a 'strong consolation' which comforts and encourages the believer. Why does hope comfort and encourage us? Because it is 'impossible for God to lie' (Heb. 6:18). Christian hope is grounded on God's faithfulness and on the trustworthiness of his Word. The people of God will know the comfort of hope when they exercise faith in the gospel of our Lord Jesus Christ. Hope comforts the heart. It is a subjective grace. Faith makes us believe, and hope makes us happy. The people of God are to lay hold of it (Heb. 6:18). God does not hope for us; no, the people of God must exercise faith in the promises of God's Word to take hold of it. Therefore, if we are feeling discouraged, we are to look to Jesus, the author and finisher of our faith, remembering 'Christ in [us], the hope of glory' (Col. 1:27). So Job anticipated God's help and rested on God's unchangeableness. Hope always looks ahead for assurance.

The source of Job's hope

Hope lives in the presence of God who is in heaven. Here it draws its vitality, life and strength. There was for Job a better hope than the old covenant because of the access he had to the Father through the Mediator (the Son). Those who believe as Job did understand that 'If in this life only we have hope in Christ, we are of all men the most pitiable' (1 Cor. 15:19). Christian hope reaches across the barrier of death and into heaven itself, the new and living way that points to the cross (Heb. 10:20). It is Christian hope that takes us to the cross, and this is where the link between faith and hope is most clearly seen (Heb. 6:19). Hope looks forward with anticipation to the fulfilment of the Bible's promises and, because of this, the people of God do not sorrow as others who have no hope (1 Thes. 4:13). This is 'the hope of His calling' (Eph. 1:18). There is, of course, such a thing as false hope, and this is acknowledged in the Book of Job (31:24; 42:9). It is found in the hearts of all who think that salvation comes to those who earn it through sacraments, good works and penances; however, the gospel is clear:

> My hope is built on nothing less
> Than Jesus' blood and righteousness;
> I dare not trust the sweetest frame
> But wholly lean on Jesus' name.[4]

> Christian hope reaches across the barrier of death and into heaven itself, the new and living way that points to the cross.

The permanent solution to our trials of testing, with their unanswered questions and pains, is to look to the Saviour and to what is promised in his Word with perseverance and hope. These will renew, sustain and strengthen faith and bring a determination not to be afraid of the future. Charles H. Spurgeon, as usual, puts it very well:

> Perhaps, O tried soul, the Lord is doing this to develop thy graces. There are some of thy graces which would never be *discovered* if it were not for thy trials. Dost thou not know that thy faith never looks so grand in summer weather as it does in winter? Hope itself is like a star—not to be seen in the sunshine of prosperity, and only to be discovered in the night of adversity. Depend upon it, God often sends us trials that our graces may be discovered, and that we may be certified of their existence. Besides, it is not merely discovery, *real growth* in grace is the result of sanctified trials. God often takes away our comforts and our privileges in order to make us better Christians.[5]

Conclusion

Job was patient with God's timing for him. He was tried and tested in bereavement, bankruptcy and illness, and Satan was behind all this, yet God allowed it for his good. How do we know it was for his good? Because the Epistle to the Romans says, 'And we know that all things work together for good to those who love God, to those who are the called according to His purpose' (8:28).

Job served God for no ulterior motive but simply because of the life of God in his soul. This is why he felt it so acutely when he was rendered useless in this task, or so he thought. He could not serve God through his family, wealth or in the strength of good health, hence his utter confusion and inward pain. This all seemed pointless. All God's children are to recognize that afflictions and trials after conversion are God's will for them. They must be like the prophets who were an example of perseverance and patience.

The Sermon on the Mount tells us, 'Blessed are you when they revile and persecute you, and say all kinds of evil against you falsely for My sake. Rejoice and be exceedingly glad, for great is your reward in heaven, for so they persecuted the prophets who were before you' (Matt .5:11–12). James says that such are happy: 'we count them blessed who endure ['persevere', *hupomeno*]' (5:11). Job was blessed when his spiritual experience was greatly enriched; his character was vindicated; he kept the faith meekly before God; and a restored life was blessed by God with prosperity and peace.

So why the Book of Job?

The aim of this book, then, is not to glorify man's innate ability to overcome suffering and stoically move on; it is instead a clear guide to God's sovereign character in his dealings with this world in terms of justice and wisdom. There is a place for innocent suffering in God's fallen world. The Book of Job is a clear guide to God's gratuitous love as seen in his commendation of Job at the beginning *and* at the end of the book, when he restores Job's blessings: 'Now the LORD blessed the latter days of Job more than his beginning' (42:12).

The doctrine of providence runs through the book, which speaks of 'all the adversity that the LORD had brought upon him' (42:11). There is no discussion of intermediate causes here, for it is understood that God was the cause of all that took place. Providence is God upholding and governing his creation in a way that fulfils his divine decrees; God is good to all, righteous in all his ways and gracious in all his works (Ps. 145:9, 17). The Westminster Confession of Faith defines providence thus:

> God the great Creator of all things does uphold, direct, dispose, and govern all creatures, actions, and things, from the greatest even to the least, by His most wise and holy providence, according to His infallible foreknowledge, and the free and immutable counsel of His own will, to the praise of the glory of His wisdom, power, justice, goodness, and mercy.
>
> God, in His ordinary providence, makes use of means, yet is free to work without, above, and against them, at His pleasure.[6]

In the words of Louis Berkhof, 'Creation is the calling into existence of that which did not exist before, while providence continues, or causes to continue, what has already been called into existence.'[7] This work of creation and providence is attributed in the New Testament to Jesus Christ: 'For by Him all things were created that are in heaven and that are on earth, visible and invisible, whether thrones or dominions or principalities or powers. All things were created through Him and for Him. And He is before all things, and in Him all things consist' (Col. 1:16–17).

All God's children are to recognize that afflictions and trials are God's will for them. They must be like the prophets, who were an example of perseverance and hope under trial. 'It is only in the riches of his grace that he permits us to sink into the depth of costly trial which enables us to be of service to him, and thus, like Job, emerge all the brighter from our trial.'[8] Christian hope is 'an anchor of the soul, both sure and steadfast, … which enters the Presence behind the veil' (Heb. 6:19). So now we see that Job's trials were for God's glory.

> When darkness veils his lovely face,
> I rest on his unchanging grace;
> In every rough and stormy gale
> My anchor holds within the veil.
> *On Christ the solid Rock I stand;*
> *All other ground is sinking sand.*[9]

FOR FURTHER STUDY

1. According to Scripture, physical sufferings, hardships and so on can be traced to moral causes: (a) Adam and the fall (Gen. 3); (b) the sins of parents (Exod. 20:5; 34:7; Deut. 5:9; 28:36; Jer. 31:29; Ezek. 18:2); (c) personal sins (Deut. 28:15–68; Jer. 31:30; Ezek. 18:4; John 5:14; Luke 13:2–3). What was the cause in Job's case?

2. What does the doctrine of perseverance teach?

3. What are the similarities and distinctions between faith and Christian hope?

TO THINK ABOUT AND DISCUSS

1. What is the best way to respond to personal suffering?

2. How does Ephesians 6:10–20 help us when we are under trial?

3. Why was the Book of Job given to us? What has most encouraged you or helped you as you have studied it?

Endnotes

Overview

1 R. L. Alden, *Job* (The New American Commentary, vol. 11; Nashville: Broadman & Holman, 1993), p. i.

2 *The Westminster Confession of Faith*, Chapter 1:4–5. See also *The Baptist Confession of Faith* 1689, Chapter 1:4.

3 Charles H. Spurgeon, *Beside Still Waters*, Roy H. Clark, ed. (Nashville: Thomas Nelson, 1999), p. 349.

Background and summary

1 Alden, *Job*, p. i.

2 Scott Noegel and Brannon Wheeler, *Historical Dictionary of Prophets in Islam and Judaism* (London/Lanham, MD: Scarecrow, 2002), p. 170.

3 Ibid., p. 171. See also A. Jeffery, 'Ayyub', in *Encyclopaedia of Islam* (Leiden: Brill, 2001).

4 Alfred Edersheim, *Bible History: Old Testament* (Peabody, MA: Hendrickson, 2001), p. 47.

5 E. J. Young, *An Introduction to the Old Testament* (Grand Rapids, MI: Eerdmans, 1970), p. 323.

6 'The hero of the book is given a patriarchal setting, authentic in detail and colouring, which has led some interpreters to suggest an early date, perhaps as early as the time of Abraham', *ESV Study Bible* (Wheaton, IL: Good News Publishers/Crossway Books, 2009; Kindle edition). Henry M. Morris says, 'It is possible that Job's experience could have occurred only 300 years or so after the flood', *The Remarkable Record of Job* (Green Forest, AR: Master Books, 2004), p. 26. See also Bodie Hodge, 'Appendix: Date of Job', *Tower of Babel* (Green Forrest, AR: Master Books, 2013).

7 Derek Thomas, *The Storm Breaks: Job Simply Explained* (Darlington: Evangelical Press, 2005), p. 14.

8 Morris, *The Remarkable Record of Job*, pp. 12–14.

Chapter 1

1 Matthew Henry, *Commentary on the Whole Bible*, vol. 3 (London: Pickering & Inglis, [n.d.]), p. 12.
2 Spurgeon, *Beside Still Waters*, p. 81.
3 Elihu's 'I also have been formed out of clay' (33:6) is a clear reference to Gen. 2:7 and the creation of Adam.
4 'Its abundant use in Job still further stresses the recognition of God as the omnipotent Creator by Job and his Semitic contemporaries', Morris, *The Remarkable Record of Job*, p. 25.
5 Pelagianism's 'fundamental proposition is: God has commanded man to do that which is good; hence the latter must have the ability to do it. This means that man has a free will in the absolute sense of the word', Louis Berkhof, *Systematic Theology* (London: Banner of Truth, 1971), pp. 232–233. Pelagianism is overwhelmingly incompatible with the Bible and was historically opposed by Augustine, Bishop of Hippo (354–430).

Chapter 2

1 George M. Philip, *Faith in the Dark* (Edinburgh: Rutherford House, 2001), p. 4.
2 David Atkinson, *The Message of Job* (Nottingham: IVP, 1991), p. 20.
3 'Old-earth creationists believe that angels have been in existence for the past 3.8 billion years or more', Hugh Ross, *Hidden Treasures in the Book of Job* (Grand Rapids, MI: Baker, 2011), p. 48. This, of course, is out of harmony with the Bible; besides, if old-earth creationism is correct, why were they not rather created when the universe was supposedly begun with the Big Bang c.14.5 billion years ago?
4 With regard to 'morning stars', 'This poetic title, given to the angels by Job, indicates their

170

intelligence, holiness and brightness of glory; excellences derived from their infinitely glorious Creator, the bright and morning star (Rev. 22)', Herbert Lockyer, *The Mystery and Ministry of Angels* (London: Parry Jackman, n.d.), p. 36.

5 Ibid., p. 14.

6 *Westminster Shorter Catechism*, answer to Question 4, 'What is God?'

Chapter 3

1 Spurgeon, *Beside Still Waters*, p. 337.

2 John Bunyan, *The Pilgrim's Progress* (London: Thomas Nelson and Sons, c.1931), p. 303.

3 Ruth Caye Jones.

Chapter 4

1 Alfred Tennyson, *In Memoriam*.

2 Fred Leahy, *Satan Cast Out* (Edinburgh: Banner of Truth, 1975), n.p.

3 Quoted in Stanley Barnes, *God Makes a Path: Daily Devotional Readings from Robert Murray M'Cheyne* (Belfast: Ambassador, 1997), p. 206.

Chapter 5

1 Morris, *The Remarkable Record of Job*, p. 43.

2 God forbids the practice of astrology (Isa. 47:12–14).

3 Jason Lisle, *The Stargazer's Guide to the Night Sky* (Green Forest, AR: Master Books, 2012), pp. 51–53, 59, 133, 166, 182.

4 *ESV Study Bible*.

Chapter 6

1 Homer Hailey, *A Commentary on Job: Now Mine Eye Seeth Thee* (Tucson, AZ: Religious Supplies Inc., 1994), p. 109.

2 R. B. Girdlestone, *Synonyms of the Old Testament* (Grand Rapids, MI: Eerdmans, 1978), pp. 76–77, 79.

3 Charles H. Spurgeon, Sermon No. 3373 on Job 16:20, published 25 September 1913 (Albany, OR: AGES Software, Version 1.0, 1997).

4 Spurgeon, Sermon No. 3373.

Chapter 7

1 Spurgeon, *Beside Still Waters*,
 p. 10.

2 Henry, *Commentary on the
 Whole Bible*, vol. 3, p. 108.

3 Francis I. Andersen, *Job: An
 Introduction and Commentary*
 (Tyndale Old Testament
 Commentaries; Nottingham:
 Inter-Varsity Press, 1976), p. 210.

4 God himself is the Redeemer of
 Israel, a fact mentioned
 nineteen times in the Old
 Testament, especially by the
 prophet Isaiah.

Chapter 8

1 Hailey, *A Commentary on Job*,
 p. 186.

2 The Hebrew translated 'circle' in
 v. 14 can also be taken as
 'sphere', William Wilson,
 *Wilson's Old Testament Word
 Studies* (McLean, VA:
 Macdonald, [n.d.]), p. 77. See
 also Isaiah 40:22. John E.
 Hartley says, 'From an ancient
 perspective, when God created
 the universe, he drew a circle to
 hold back the heavenly waters

from covering the earth (Prov.
8:27). His abode is located
above this circle', *The Book of
Job* (Grand Rapids, MI:
Eerdmans, 1988), p. 329. This
interpretation of ancient Near
Eastern cosmology is not certain
to be accurate. So we must
beware of anything that takes
away from the inspiration of the
Book of Job as well as from the
clear teaching of Genesis about
creation in six days. Jesus said,
'Your word is truth' (John
17:17). Peter Enns, who has
gone astray in this matter,
writes, 'Genesis—as other
stories of the ancient
world—thus portrays the world
as a flat disc with a dome
above. Below the earth were
the waters threatening to gush
up, and above the dome were
the waters threatening to drop
down (see Gen. 7:11). The
biblical world view described in
Genesis is an ancient Near
Eastern one', *Inspiration and
Incarnation* (Grand Rapids, MI:
Baker Academic, 2009), p. 54.

See Morris, *The Remarkable Record of Job*, pp. 42–43, for a critique of Enns's view.

3 Hailey, *A Commentary on Job*, p. 209.

4 Spurgeon, *Beside Still Waters*, p. 72.

5 William F. Lloyd, 1824.

Chapter 9

1 'Fifteen or more facts of science are suggested in Job that scientists did not discover until recent centuries. Another number of such anticipations of modern science are scattered throughout the Bible, but Job probably contains more than any other one book', Morris, *The Remarkable Record of Job*, p. 35.

2 Ibid., p. 40.

3 See http://hyperphysics. phy-astr.gsu.edu/hbase/orbv. html for information on gravity and the earth's orbit.

4 'Apollo 8, the second manned mission in the United States Apollo space program, was launched on December 21, 1968, and became the first manned spacecraft to leave Earth orbit, reach the Earth's Moon, orbit it and return safely to Earth', 'Apollo 8', at http:// en.wikipedia.org/wiki/ Apollo_8.

Chapter 10

1 Hartley, *The Book of Job*, p. 429.

2 See David C. Hester, *Job* (Louisville, KY: Westminster John Knox, 2005); Gary Benfold, *Why Lord? The Book of Job for Today* (Epsom: Day One, 1998).

3 For those who see Elihu as a Spirit-led man, see Hartley, *The Book of Job*; Peter Williams, *From Despair to Hope* (Epsom: Day One, 2002). For those who see him otherwise, see Morris, *The Remarkable Record of Job*; Philip, *Faith in the Dark*. For a fuller discussion of the ideas involved, see William Henry Green, *Conflict and Triumph: The Argument of the Book of Job Unfolded* (Edinburgh: Banner of Truth, 1999), pp. 123–136.

4 'The fact that the text states four times that Elihu became angry (vv. 2, 3, 5) cues us in on the quality of his speeches', C. Hassell Bullock, *An Introduction to the Old Testament Poetic Books* (Chicago: Moody, 1988), p. 124.

Chapter 11

1 Morris, *The Remarkable Record of Job*, p. 47. See also pp. 105–106 on this topic.

2 It is always best to distinguish between the questions 'What is God?' and 'Who is God?' for a clearer understanding of God's nature and grace.

3 Charles H. Spurgeon, Sermon No. 1146 on Psalm 31:22 (Albany, OR: AGES Software, Version 1.0, 1997).

4 See my commentary *Opening up Colossians and Philemon* (Leominster: Day One, 2006), pp. 70–80.

Chapter 12

1 Andersen, *Job*, p. 311.

2 'Some dinosaurs walked holding their tails parallel, stiff as a beam. Job recorded only what an eyewitness account of the living creature could deliver', Isaacs, *Dragons or Dinosaurs*, p. 161.

3 Dinosaurs are only a mystery if you accept the evolutionary time line of billions of years. There is no mystery if you accept that the fossil record reveals animals that God created on the sixth day of the creation account. 'American biologist professor Roy Mackal has boldly stated that, in his opinion, Behemoth might be an undiscovered species of living long-necked dinosaur, similar to *Diplodocus* and *Apatosaurus*. Such a beast would certainly resemble the Bible's description of Behemoth', Karl Shuker, *Dragons: A Natural History* (London: Aurum, 1995), p. 37.

4 A. Barnes, *Notes on the Old Testament: Isaiah*, vol. 1 (Grand Rapids, MI: Baker, 1972), p. 413. Genesis 1:21 declares, 'So God created great sea

174

creatures'; the Hebrew word translated 'great sea creatures' is actually the word for 'dragon', Ken Ham, *The Great Dinosaur Mystery Solved!*(Green Forest, AR: Master Books, 2002), p. 47.

5 Ham, *The Great Dinosaur Mystery Solved!*, p. 43.

6 Andersen, *Job*, p. 312.

7 Under the headline 'Skull of Huge Sea Monster that Could Have Eaten *T. rex* Found in Dorset', *The Times* reported the discovery of an 'eight-foot-long (2.4 m) skull [that] belonged to a pliosaur, an aquatic reptile reminiscent of the dinosaurs but with four fins, powerful necks, and sharp teeth. And if the creature's body is proportional to the size of its skull, it will be one of the largest pliosaur fossils ever found— perhaps some 54 feet (16 m) long, having originally weighed between 7 and 13 tons. Palaeontologists hope to examine the cliff further to see if the rest of the fossil is buried inside, but that project could take decades, warns Dorset earth science manager Richard Edmonds', 31 October 2009; quoted at http://www.answersingenesis.org/articles/2009/10/31/news-to-note-10312009.8

8 'This is correctly rendered, and refers to the fact that the monster here referred to throws itself into immense volumes or folds, a description that applies to all serpents of all sizes', A. Barnes, *Notes on the Old Testament: Isaiah*, vol. 1, p. 415.

9 Ibid., p. 414.

Chapter 13

1 *Westminster Shorter Catechism*, answer to Question 35, 'What is sanctification?'

2 Andersen, *Job*, p. 316.

Chapter 14

1 Quoted in Barnes, *God Makes a Path*, p. 91.

2 W. E. Vine, *Expository Dictionary of Bible Words* (Basingstoke: Marshall,

Morgan & Scott, 1985), vol. 2,
p. 29; vol. 3, p. 12.

3 Souter, *A Pocket Lexicon*, 1960.

4 Edward Mote, c.1834.

5 C. H. Spurgeon, *Morning & Evening*, 18 February (McLean, VA: MacDonald, n.d.).

6 *The Westminster Confession of Faith*, Chapter 5:1, 3.

7 Berkhof, *Systematic Theology*, p. 167.

8 William Still, *Through the Year: A Book of Daily Readings*, D. C. Searle, ed. (Edinburgh: Banner of Truth/Rutherford House), 2006, p. 275.

9 Edward Mote, 'My Hope Is Built on Nothing Less', c.1834.

Additional resources

Alden, R. L, *Job* (The New American Commentary, vol. 11; Nashville: Broadman & Holman, 1993)

Benfold, Gary, *Why Lord? The Book of Job for Today* (Epsom: Day One, 1998)

Bullock, C. Hassell, *An Introduction to the Old Testament Poetic Books* (Chicago: Moody, 1988)

Edersheim, Alfred, *Bible History: Old Testament* (Peabody, MA: Hendrickson, 2001)

Green, William Henry, *Conflict and Triumph: The Argument of the Book of Job Unfolded* (Edinburgh: Banner of Truth, 1999)

Hailey, Homer, *A Commentary on Job: Now Mine Eye Seeth Thee* (Tucson, AZ: Religious Supply 1994)

Hartley, John E., *The Book of Job* (Grand Rapids, MI: Eerdmans, 1988)

Hodge, Bodie, 'Appendix: Date of Job', in *Tower of Babel* (Green Forest, AR: Master Books, 2013)

Morris, Henry M., *The Remarkable Record of Job* (Green Forest, AR: Master Books, 2004)

Philip, George M., *Faith in the Dark* (Edinburgh: Rutherford House, 2001)

Thomas, Derek, *The Storm Breaks: Job Simply Explained* (Darlington: Evangelical Press, 2005)

Williams, Peter, *From Despair to Hope* (Epsom: Day One, 2002)